basic blueprint reading and sketching

basic blueprint reading and sketching

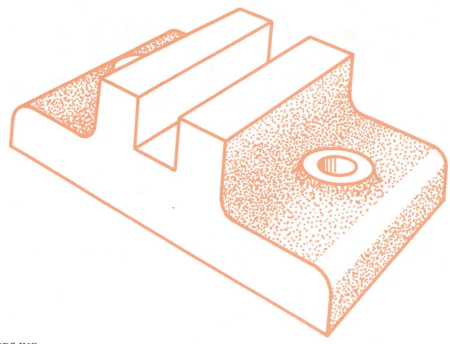

10 9 8 7 6

LIBRARY OF CONGRESS CATALOG CARD NUMBER: 76-56490
ISBN: 0-8273-2050-7 Softcover
ISBN: 08273-2141-4 Hardcover

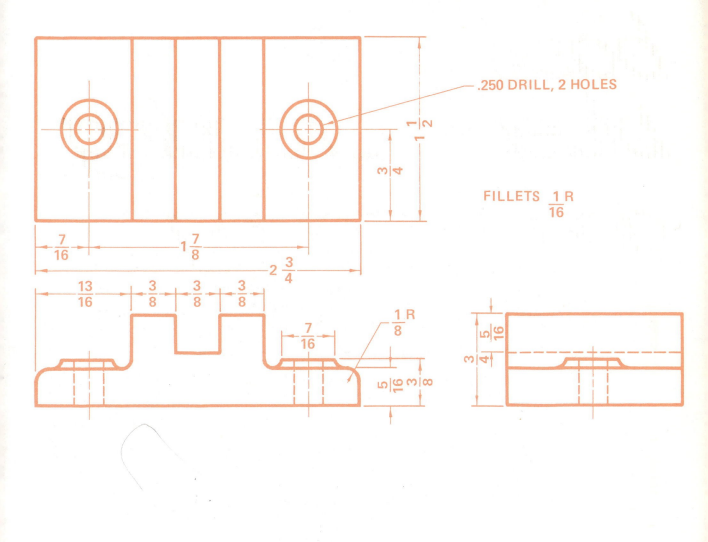

.250 DRILL, 2 HOLES

FILLETS $\frac{1}{16}$ R

DR. C. THOMAS OLIVO • ALBERT V. PAYNE • THOMAS P. OLIVO

DELMAR PUBLISHERS INC. • ALBANY, NEW YORK 12205

FOREWORD

BASIC BLUEPRINT READING AND SKETCHING is the basic text-workbook in a series which provides instructional material and practical applications for students, apprentices, technicians, and others who must develop the ability to read and interpret blueprints, and make simple sketches.

This edition of BASIC BLUEPRINT READING AND SKETCHING has been updated in content. The format still includes the use of two colors throughout the text to assist the student to understand and apply each new principle or concept as it is introduced.

The new content reflects the latest trends in drafting conventions, shop and industrial practices, and the increasing trend for conversion from the English system of measurement to the metric system. The following list summarizes the changes and additions to the text.

Unit 1   Coverage of print reproduction methods was expanded and updated.

Unit 22   This NEW unit describes datums and illustrates ordinate and tabular dimensioning. These principles and techniques are applied in the interpretation of a typical numerical control drawing.

Unit 26   This NEW unit introduces first-angle projection techniques used in the metric system and the metric dimensioning of fractional values.

Unit 38   This NEW unit demonstrates pictorial plane (aligned) and unidirectional dimensioning practices. The pictorial sketch in isometric covers applications of metric dimensions.

An Instructor's Guide is available for BASIC BLUEPRINT READING AND SKETCHING. The answers and drawings required for all assignments in the text-workbook are presented in the Guide. Answers are provided in the same format as that used on the assignment pages of the text to allow the instructor to check completed assignments quickly and accurately.

Once the fundamental principles given in BASIC BLUEPRINT READING AND SKETCHING have been mastered, and an ability to interpret blueprints has been demonstrated, the student can proceed to a study of the more advanced text-workbooks. BLUEPRINT READING FOR MACHINISTS – INTERMEDIATE, BLUEPRINT READING FOR MACHINISTS – ADVANCED, and INTERPRETING ENGINEERING DRAWINGS present more advanced drafting principles to further develop the interpretative ability of the student.

BLUEPRINT READING FOR MACHINISTS — INTERMEDIATE

Principles of Projection, Positions of Views, Finished Surface Symbol; Making Sketches; Arrangement of Views, Revolved Sections; Partial Sections, Locating Cutting Planes; Section Lining, Conventional Sectioning, Partial Views; Scale Drawings; Baseline Dimensioning, Point-to-Point Dimensioning; Representation of Screw Threads, Classification of Fits, Thread Symbols; Identifying Steels; Representation of Pipe Threads; Drilling, Reaming, Boring; Dovetails; Molding; Irregular or Odd-Shaped Castings; Auxiliary Views, Phantom Outlines, Structural Steel Shapes, Finishes; Taper Pins, Dowel Pins, Cotter Pins; Worms, Worm Gears, Splines; Coil Springs; Swivels; Universal Joints; Boring Split Bearings, Machining Lugs.

BLUEPRINT READING FOR MACHINISTS — ADVANCED

Phantom Lines, Dimensioning, and Bottom Views; Special Sections; Special Methods of Showing Combined Sections; Auxiliary Section Views; Assembly Drawings; Combined Assembly and Detail Drawings; Partially Detailed Assembly Drawings; Specification of Parts; Construction or Working Assembly Drawings; Pictorial Assembly Drawings; Representation of Special Features of a Design; Multiscale Drawings; Drawings with Complex Parts; Cams; Spur Gearing; Bevel Gears; Worm Gears; Die Casting.

BASIC BLUEPRINT READING AND SKETCHING is a prerequisite to the study of INTER-PRETING ENGINEERING DRAWINGS by Jensen and Hines. This comprehensive text-workbook uses the latest drafting conventions and shop practices to provide blueprint reading experience with an emphasis on current industrial needs.

INTERPRETING ENGINEERING DRAWINGS

Third-Angle Projection, Visible Object Lines, Lettering; Working Drawings, Dimensions; Hidden Lines; Sloping Surfaces, Measurement of Angles; Scale Drawings, Rounds and Fillets, Machine Slots; Circular Features, Dimensioning Cylindrical Features and Holes, Drilling, Reaming, Boring; Break Lines, Not-to-Scale Dimensions, Machining Symbols; Sectional Views, Countersinks, Counterbores, Spot-faces; One and Two View Drawings, Chamfering, Necking, Detail Drawings; Tolerances and Allowances; Thread Representation, Knurls; Revolved and Removed Sections; Keys, Flats, Bosses and Pads, Drawing Revisions; Arrowless Dimensioning, Tabular Dimensioning; Steel Specifications; Castings; Dovetails; Auxiliary Views; Bearings; Arrangement of Views; Broken Out and Partial Sections; Pin Fasteners; Point-to-Point Dimensioning; Assembly Drawings, Bills of Materials; Conventional Sectioning of Webs, Helical Spring, Pipe Threads; International Organization for Standardization, Metric Dimensioning; Structural Steel Shapes; Machining Lugs, Finishes; Welding Drawings, Fillet Welds, Groove Welds, Cams; Gears, Spur Gears; Bevel Gears; Gear Trains; True Position Dimensioning, Geometrical Tolerancing; Rolling Element Bearings, Retaining Rings, O-Ring Seals; Clutches, Belt Drives.

PREFACE

Blueprints are the guideposts of industry. Using blueprints, both simple and complex parts and mechanisms can be described graphically with such completeness that one part, or any number of the same part, can be manufactured to the specified size, shape, and degree of accuracy. The blueprint points the way at each stage of production from the time an idea is conceived until the product is completed.

If it were possible to accumulate all blueprints produced over a long period of years, they would furnish an accurate inventory of manufactured articles and experimental projects. These blueprints would represent a partial historical record of the achievements and progress of civilization.

They would tell another story, too, about intercountry dependence and cooperation, since the blueprint is the universal language of industry. While systems of measurements and drafting techniques vary between different countries, there is an accelerating movement toward standardization. The International System of Units (SI), established by agreement among nations, provides the interlocking framework for greater acceptance of the metric system of measurement. The International Organization for Standardization (ISO) is also active in trying to establish standards that are acceptable throughout the world. During the many years to come of conversion from the American/British units of measurement to the metric system, individuals who can interpret drawings will be able to produce identical parts and mechanisms even though they work in different lands. The universal language of the blueprint forms the foundation for the production of interchangeable parts.

Because techniques of representation differ with manufacturers, it was necessary to make careful analyses of drafting room practices and occupational studies to determine the blueprint reading needs of skilled and semiskilled workers. These comparative studies of training needs provided direction and emphasized the degree of thoroughness with which each instructional unit of this text had to be organized and written.

Recommended standards of the American National Standards Institute (ANSI) and the International Organization of Standards are used in this edition of BASIC BLUEPRINT READING AND SKETCHING. Additional units are included to illustrate how the metric system of measurement is applied to drawings. The scope of the instructional units in this text insures complete mastery of blueprint reading by the student. The units cover the range of drawings, sketches, and prints which technicians and mechanics are normally required to read and interpret accurately. The individual units incorporate many of the newest, tested teaching-learning methods and curriculum development practices which the writers have used successfully under actual conditions.

Grateful acknowledgment is made to Elmer A. Rotmans, former Head of the Drafting Department, Edison Technical and Industrial High School, Rochester, New York, for the skillful preparation of the drawings; and to Peter J. Olivo, former Associate Director of Curriculum Research, Delmar Publishers.

Dr. C. Thomas Olivo
Albert V. Payne
Thomas P. Olivo

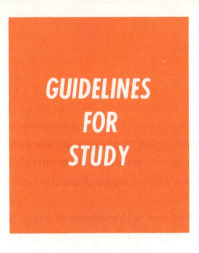

GUIDELINES FOR STUDY

BASIC BLUEPRINT READING AND SKETCHING is divided into two major parts. Part One covers the basic principles of blueprint reading and provides the student with applications of each new principle. Part Two deals with the techniques of making shop sketches without the use of instruments.

In each part, the units are grouped in sections. Part One begins with an Introduction to Blueprint Reading followed by Section 1 on Lines; Section 2, Views; Section 3, Dimensions and Notes; Section 4, Sections; and Section 5, The Metric and International Systems. Part Two contains Section 6 on Shop Sketching.

The instructional units in both parts are arranged in a natural sequence of teaching-learning difficulty. Each instructional unit includes a Basic Principle, a Blueprint, and an Assignment.

Basic Principle Series

In the Basic Principle Series, drafting principles and concepts and all the related technical information necessary to interpret each new item on a drawing are described in detail. Terminology, shop, and laboratory practices are defined and applied in operational notes of the type normally appearing on drawings. The topics in this series are arranged in the logical order of dependence of one basic principle on the next.

Blueprint Series

Each new basic principle is applied on one or more industrial blueprints. Certain changes have been made from the original drawings to provide a wide range of experiences through the use of different drafting techniques. Many of the shop and laboratory drawings for the beginning units have been simplified by removing the title blocks. The drawings are prepared according to the latest accepted standards established by the American National Standards Institute (ANSI). In some instances, the standards of the International Organization for Standardization (ISO) are used.

Assignment Series

In the Assignment Series, questions and problems are provided to cover the application of the basic principles on the drawings or blueprints for each unit. Sufficient repetition is provided to insure the mastery of each new basic principle. The questions use typical shop terminology and are intended to develop and test the student's ability to read shop drawings and blueprints for required dimensions, shape descriptions, machining operations, and other essential data. This is the kind of information which is needed by the technician or craftsperson for the layout, fabrication, construction, assembly, testing, or operation of a single part or a mechanism of many parts.

Encircled letters and numbers are used throughout the Blueprint and Assignment Series to simplify the problems which otherwise would require lengthy, time-consuming descriptions. A ruled space is included on each assignment sheet for solutions to all problem material.

PART TWO, SHOP SKETCHING

The organization of the units in this section is identical to that of the units in Part One. The first units cover the principles of sketching simple straight and slant lines, curved lines, circles, and rounded corners and edges. These different shapes of lines are combined in sketching more complicated parts.

The methods of straight lettering and slant lettering, with either the right or left hand, are covered in two units as there is daily need for lettering and dimensioning. The last five units in the section deal with the techniques of making orthographic, oblique, isometric and perspective sketches, and pictorial drawings with dimensioning.

Within each unit, a few practical, simplified techniques of sketching are described and illustrated. These are followed by a blueprint which either shows how the techniques are applied to shop sketches or furnishes information from which the student makes sketches, without the use of drafting instruments or equipment.

A current catalog including prices of all Delmar educational publications is available upon request. Please write to:

Catalog Department
Delmar Publishers Inc.
50 Wolf Road
Albany, New York 12205

CONTENTS

PART 1

Section 1   LINES

Section 2   VIEWS

Section 3   DIMENSIONS AND NOTES

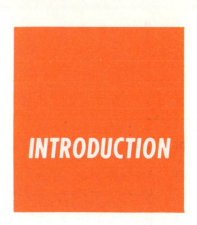

INTRODUCTION

UNIT **1** *BASES FOR INTERPRETING BLUEPRINTS AND SKETCHES*

Technical information about the shape and construction of a simple part may be conveyed from one person to another by the spoken or written word.   As the addition of details makes the part or mechanism more and more complex, the designer, draftsperson, engineer, and mechanic must use precise methods to describe the object adequately.

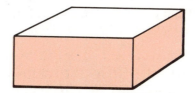

FIGURE 1-1 A PICTURE OF A RECTANGULAR BLOCK

Although a picture of a part, figure 1-1, or a photograph will help in describing an object, neither method shows the exact sizes, cutaway sections, or machining operations required.   On the other hand, the blueprint of a drawing made accurately with instruments or a shop sketch meets the requirements for an accurate description of shape, construction and size, figure 1-2.

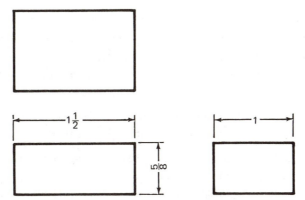

FIGURE 1-2 MECHANICAL DRAWING OF THE RECTANGULAR BLOCK

BLUEPRINT READING AS A UNIVERSAL LANGUAGE

Blueprints are the universal language by which all the information the mechanic, designer, and others need to know is furnished.   Blueprint reading refers to the process of interpreting a print to form a mental picture of how the object looks when completed.

Training in blueprint reading includes the development of the ability to visualize various manufacturing or fabricating processes required to make the part, certain basic principles underlying the use of various types of lines and views, how to apply dimensions, and how the inside of a part looks in section. The mechanic must develop an understanding of the universal standards, symbols, signs, and other techniques which the draftsperson uses to describe a part, unit or mechanism completely. Technicians also develop fundamental skills in making sketches so that with pencil and paper they can record the data on the sketch relating to dimensions, notes and other details needed to construct the part.

INDUSTRIAL PRACTICES RELATING TO THE USE OF DRAWINGS

In modern industrial practice, original drawings are seldom sent to the shop or laboratory. Instead, exact reproductions of the original are made. The duplicate copies are then distributed to all individuals, departments, and plants who are responsible for planning, fabricating, or assembling a part or unit. The original drawings are filed for record purposes and for protection. Revisions and changes in design are often recorded on these drawings.

Master drawings may be made freehand, with the aid of drafting instruments, or by combining hand processes with the use of acetate sheets. These sheets are available commercially with preprinted lines, symbols and other standard parts and information. When the required item is removed from the acetate sheet, positioned and stuck to the base material, it becomes a part of the original drawing.

Many industries translate statistical and other data by using computers which feed and control automated drafting machines. These machines may be used to produce original drawings or to draw complicated shapes or circuits directly on parts that are to be machined, formed, or assembled into simple or complex units.

REPRODUCTION PROCESSES

Reproduction is the process of making one or more copies of a drawing, sketch, or other written material. A reproduction may be made to the same size as the original, or it may be an enlargement or a reduction of the original size. The reproduction may also be in a positive form like the master, or in a negative form in which light and dark areas are reversed from the master.

There are five basic reproduction processes in common use. Each process yields a particular kind of print. The kind of print depends on such requirements as time and cost factors, resistance to soiling and aging under specific work conditions, size, quantity, and desirable color.

The five basic processes may be classified as: (1) the iron process, (2) electrostatic process, (3) silver process, (4) diazo process, and (5) heat process.

The common materials used for the original drawings from which reproductions are made include paper, cloth, polyester or acetate film, aluminum foil, metal, and glass. The accompanying chart shows the basic reproduction processes and the materials on which drawings can be made for each process.

The Blueprint/Brownprint Iron Process

One of the oldest and still widely used practical and inexpensive processes of duplicating master drawings is called *blueprinting*. In reproducing drawings by this method, the blueprint is made on a paper or cloth coated with an emulsion which is sensitive to light. A transparent tracing of the required drawing is placed on the sensitized paper or cloth. When exposed to a strong light which passes through the transparent tracing, the lines on the drawing hold back some of the light and leave their impression on the blueprint paper. After exposure to a light source, the sensitized paper or cloth is passed through a developer, washed with water, fixed by an oxidizing agent, rewashed, and dried. The blueprint, except for slight shrinkage during the drying process, is an exact duplicate, in negative form, of the original drawing.

Basic Reproduction Processes		Basic Materials of Original Drawings				
		Paper	Cloth	Film: Polyester/ Acetate	Metal/ Glass	Foil: Aluminum
A	Iron Process (Blue/Brown print)	X	X			
B	Electrostatic Process (Xeroxing)	X				X
C	Silver Process (Photocopying)	X	X	X	X	X
D	Diazo Process (White/Sepia print)	X	X	X		X
E	Heat Process (Blue/Black print)	X				

For example, on the original drawing of the Guide Pin, the lines and dimensions are black or opaque on a transparent background material. The print of the Guide Pin, figure 1-3, is the negative of the original; that is, the lines are white on a color background.

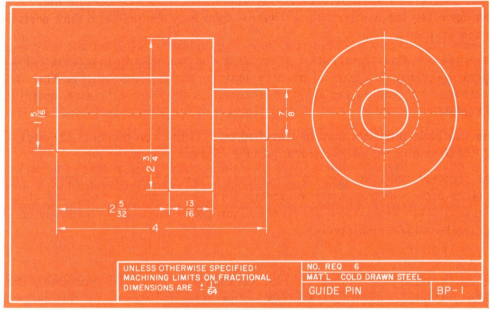

FIGURE 1-3 SAMPLE BLUEPRINT

It should also be noted that figure 1-3 includes a *title block* in the lower, right-hand corner. A title block may contain such information as:

- Name of the part
- Quantity needed
- Order number
- Date
- Number of the drawing

- Scale size used
- Name of draftsperson
- Name of drawing inspector
- Material

The term *blueprint,* was originally meant to refer to a blue and white reproduction. Today it is used loosely in modern industrial language to cover many different kinds of reproductions. *Brownprints* are produced by a similar process using a coating that, after exposure to light and washing in a hypo bath, causes the paper to turn a deep brown-black. The brownprint copy is translucent and may be used as a negative master from which the same or other kinds of prints may be made.

The Electrostatic Process

In the electrostatic process a base material of paper or metal, coated with zinc oxide, is given an electrostatic charge. The original to be reproduced is either projected or brought into contact with the coating. Ultraviolet light is used. The electrostatic charge is eliminated in all areas except those which are shadowed by the markings on the original. As a result, the base material is left with an invisible electrostatic image of the original.

An electrostatically charged powder, with a charge opposite to the zinc oxide, is dusted over the base material. The powder particles adhere to the areas that still contain charged zinc oxide. When the original base material is translucent, the print is made permanent by heat fusion. Otherwise, the image of the original must be transferred to a translucent or offset plate.

The electrostatic process can be used also to produce *mats.* The mats serve as plates for offset printing. This method of reproducing large quantities of drawings and other technical data is fast and economical.

The portable telecopier is another application of the electrostatic process. The telecopier makes volume prints from original drawings or microfilm. The telecopier can also receive or send design, engineering, production, and other technical information contained on prints over standard telephone lines. Once a telephone circuit is established, the receivers are placed in position on the telecopier. The document is fed into the transmitting machine. The receiving machine converts the input signals into an exact reproduction of the original copy.

The Silver Process

The silver process is the oldest reproduction process and is better recognized under the names of *photostat®, photocopy,* and *microfilm.* In each case, the reproduction is made using photographic processes and materials.

Permanently enlarged or reduced reproductions of drawings, or any other master copy, may be made on any base material that can be coated with a sensitized solution, photographed, washed, fixed in another solution for permanence, and dried.

Since there are many variations of the silver process, it is possible to produce a positive print from a positive original, a negative print from a positive, or prints using a number of other combinations. The sensitized materials may be exposed by direct contact with the master, by having a light pass through the original, or by bouncing light from the original back to the sensitized coating.

A microfilm is a photographically reduced copy. The microfilm is used internationally to record drawings and other significant information at a fraction of the actual size. The original copy is reduced up to 60 times. The photographed image appears on a roll of film or it may be placed individually in an aperture card.

Microfilm systems are built around four basic sizes: 16 mm, 35 mm, 70 mm, and 105 mm. The microfilm is read on a special enlarging reader for rapid viewing and legibility. Enlargements can be made electrostatically, photographically, or by photocopying processes. Reproduction of prints from microfilm is rapid. Copies may be produced automatically and in a variety of sizes.

There are many advantages to a microfilming system. There is a limited amount of space required for the storage of drawings, prints, and other data. Microfilming also helps to preserve original drawings and provides for easy reference and location. The system can easily be locked into a computer bank.

Since the aperture card is essentially a standard data card, specific information can be punched into it. Thus, it is possible to sort, file, and retrieve aperture cards according to the specific information required. Duplicate cards and/or reproductions of a desired drawing may then be produced.

The Diazo Process

Positive-reading reproductions with dark lines of almost any color on a white background can be produced by the diazo process. In the dry diazo process, the dark areas of a drawing prevent a sensitized material from being exposed to an ultraviolet light. Exposure of the print material to an ammonia atmosphere develops the color in the unexposed area. *Sepia* (yellow-brown) prints or prints with other colors may be made by varying the azo dye composition.

Wet whiteprints or sepia prints are similar to the dry prints except that a wet solution is used after exposure and the reproductions require drying. Reproductions by the diazo process are not as permanent as those resulting from other processes. The print may fade over a period of time.

The Heat Process

The heat process produces changes in heat-sensitive chemicals that are used to coat a base material. Dark areas on a drawing permit more heat to be absorbed by the sensitized coating than do unmarked areas. As a result, the additional heat absorbed by the chemically-treated base material produces a blue-black reproduction which is a positive print of the original.

Regardless of the method of duplicating an original drawing, the principles of graphically describing an object to furnish exact and positive information remain the same. Again, blueprint reading refers to the process of interpreting a drawing by visualizing the object clearly, accurately, and with speed and skill from the information which is presented in graphic form.

ELEMENTS COMMON TO ALL DRAWINGS

A mechanical drawing includes lines of different lengths, shapes, and intensity. These lines, when combined with each other, define the form, details, and size of an object. The lines in turn are grouped according to the surfaces of the object being viewed in what are called *views*. As a further help in describing the object, certain dimensions and notes are included on each view. Sometimes objects are cut apart by imaginary cutting planes to show a *sectional view* of the internal shape and construction of the part.

The fundamental principles of blueprint reading by which typical industrial drawings can be interpreted are included in the instructional units in the following sections: Section 1, Lines; Section 2, Views; Section 3, Dimensions and Notes; Section 4, Sections; and Section 5, The Metric and International Systems. The basic elements of making freehand sketches are covered in the units in Section 6.

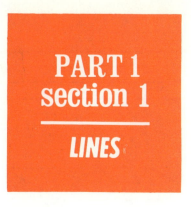
UNIT **2**   *THE ALPHABET OF LINES, OBJECT LINES*

The line is the basis of all industrial drawings. By combining lines of different thicknesses, types, and lengths, it is possible to describe graphically any object in sufficient detail so that a craftsperson with a basic understanding of blueprint reading can accurately visualize the shape of the part.

THE ALPHABET OF LINES

The American National Standards Institute (ANSI) has adopted and recommended certain drafting techniques and standards for lines. The types of lines commonly found on drawings are known as the *alphabet of lines.* The six types of lines which are most widely used from this alphabet include: (1) object lines, (2) hidden lines, (3) center lines, (4) extension lines, (5) dimension lines, and (6) projection lines. A brief description and examples of each of the six types of lines are given in this unit. These lines are used in combination with each other on all the prints in the Blueprint Series. Problem material on the identification of lines is included in the Assignment Series.

The weights of lines are relative because they depend largely on the size of the drawing and the complexity of each member of an object. For this reason, comparative weights of lines are used.

OBJECT LINES

The shape of an object is described on a drawing by heavy lines known as visible edge or object lines. An object line, figure 2-1, is always drawn heavy and solid so that the outline or shape of the object is clearly emphasized on the drawing, figure 2-2.

(SOLID, HEAVY LINE) — THIS TYPE OF LINE REPRESENTS THE OUTLINE OF AN OBJECT. THICKNESS OF THE LINE MAY VARY ACCORDING TO THE SIZE AND COMPLEXITY OF THE PART BEING DESCRIBED.

FIGURE 2-1 OBJECT LINE

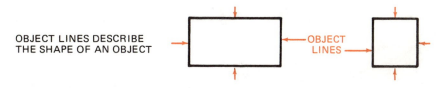

OBJECT LINES DESCRIBE THE SHAPE OF AN OBJECT

OBJECT LINES

FIGURE 2-2 APPLICATION OF THE OBJECT LINE

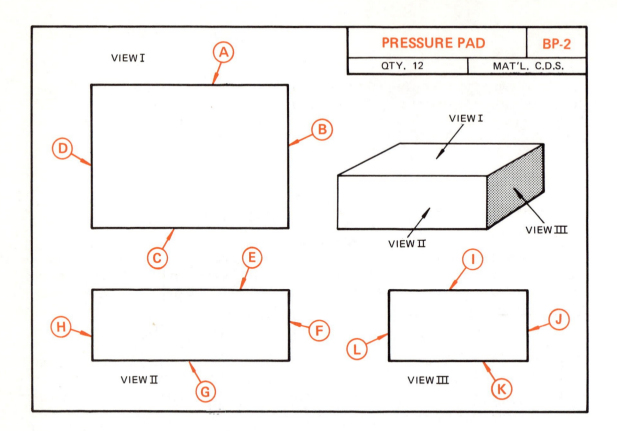

PRESSURE PAD (BP-2)

1. Give the name of the part.

2. What is the number of the blueprint?

3. How many Pressure Pads are needed?

4. What name is given to the heavy line which shows the shape of the part?

5. What lettered lines show the shape of the part in:

    a. View I

    b. View II

    c. View III

ASSIGNMENT   UNIT 2

Student's Name _____

1. _____

2. _____

3. _____

4. _____

5. View I _____

   View II _____

   View III _____

UNIT 3

HIDDEN LINES, CENTER LINES

HIDDEN LINES

To be complete, a drawing must include lines which represent all the edges and intersections of surfaces in the object. Many of these lines are invisible to the observer because they are covered by other portions of the object. To show that a line is hidden, the draftsperson usually uses a series of short dashes, figure 3-1. Figure 3-2 illustrates the use of hidden lines.

(MEDIUM WEIGHT, SHORT DASHES) THIS TYPE OF LINE REPRESENTS INVISIBLE EDGES AND SURFACES

FIGURE 3-1 HIDDEN LINES

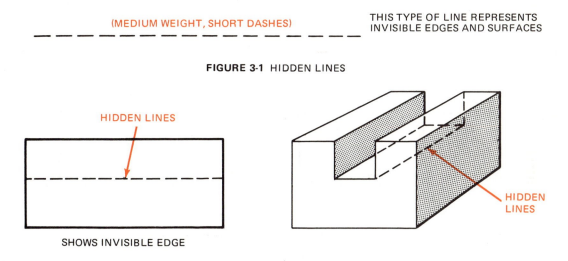

SHOWS INVISIBLE EDGE

FIGURE 3-2 APPLICATION OF HIDDEN LINES

CENTER LINES

A center line, figure 3-3, is drawn as a light broken line of long and short dashes, spaced alternately. Center lines are used to indicate the center of a whole circle or a part of a circle, and also to show that an object is symmetrical about a line, figure 3-4.

(LIGHTWEIGHT, LONG AND SHORT DASHES) THIS TYPE OF LINE INDICATES CENTERS OF CIRCLES, ARCS, AND SYMMETRICAL OBJECTS

FIGURE 3-3 CENTER LINES

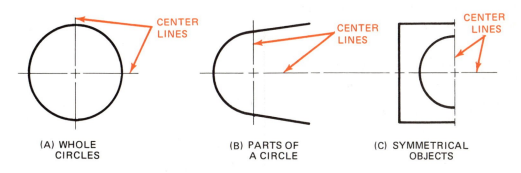

(A) WHOLE CIRCLES (B) PARTS OF A CIRCLE (C) SYMMETRICAL OBJECTS

FIGURE 3-4 APPLICATION OF CENTER LINES

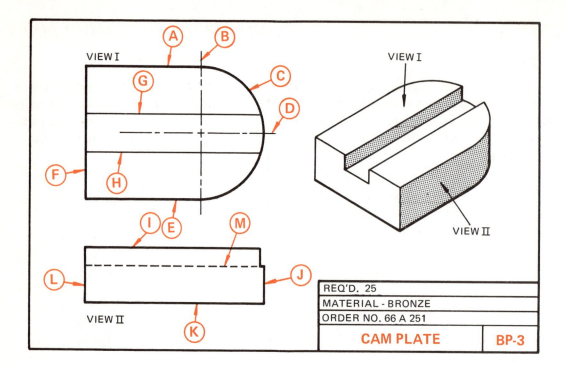

REQ'D. 25
MATERIAL - BRONZE
ORDER NO. 66 A 251

CAM PLATE   **BP-3**

CAM PLATE (BP-3)

1. How many Cam Plates are required?

2. Name the material for the parts.

3. What type of line is used to describe the shape of the part?

4. Give the letters of all the lines which show the outside shape of the part.

5. Name the kind of line which represents an invisible edge.

6. What lettered lines in View I show the slot in the Cam Plate?

7. What line in View II shows an invisible surface?

8. What kind of line indicates the center of a circle, or part of a circle?

9. What lettered line in View I shows the circular end?

10. What lettered lines in View I are used to locate the center of the circular end?

ASSIGNMENT   UNIT 3
Student's Name _____

1. _____

2. _____

3. _____

4. _____

5. _____

6. _____

7. _____

8. _____

9. _____

10. _____

EXTENSION LINES, DIMENSION LINES

EXTENSION LINES

Extension lines are used in dimensioning to show the size of an object. Extension lines, figure 4-1, are light, solid lines which extend away from an object at the exact places between which dimensions are to be placed.

FIGURE 4-1 EXTENSION LINES
USED FOR DIMENSIONS.

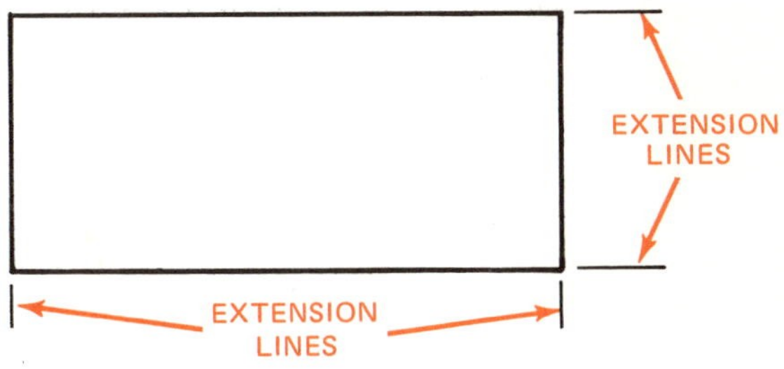

FIGURE 4-2 APPLICATION OF EXTENSION LINES
IN DIMENSIONING

A space of one-sixteenth inch is usually allowed between the object and the beginning of the extension line, figure 4-2.

DIMENSION LINES

Dimension lines, figure 4-3, are light, solid lines with arrowheads at each end. The tips or points of these arrowheads indicate the exact distance referred to by a dimension placed at a break in the line.

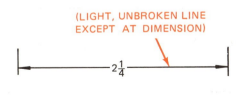

FIGURE 4-3 DIMENSION LINE

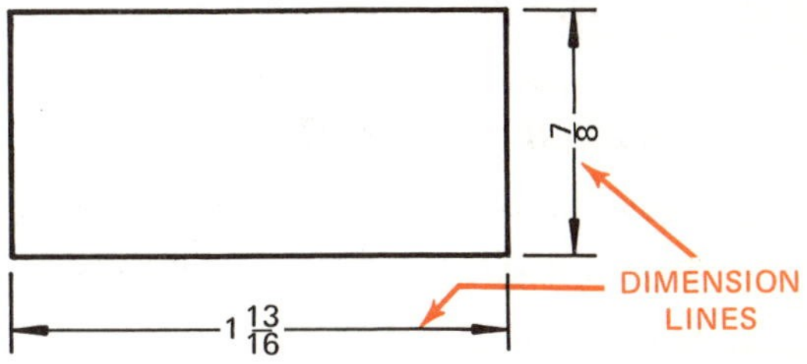

FIGURE 4-4 APPLICATION OF
DIMENSION LINES

The point or tip of the arrowhead touches the extension line. The size of the arrow is determined by the weight of the dimension line and the size of the drawing. Closed (———) and open (———) arrowheads are the two shapes generally used. The extension line, figure 4-4, usually projects 1/16 inch beyond a dimension line. Any additional length to the extension line is of no value in dimensioning.

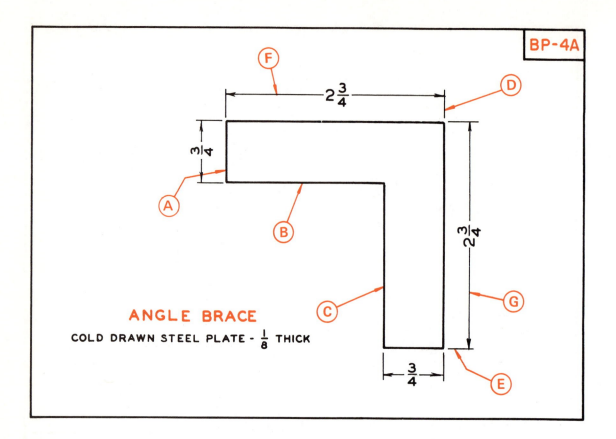

BP-4A

ANGLE BRACE

COLD DRAWN STEEL PLATE - $\frac{1}{8}$ THICK

ANGLE BRACE (BP-4A)

1. Name the material specified for the Angle Brace.

2. What is the overall length of each side of the Brace?

3. What is the width of each leg of the Brace?

4. What is the thickness of the metal in the Brace?

5. What is the name given to the kind of line marked (A) , (B) , and (C) ?

6. What kind of lines are (D) and (E) ?

7. What kind of lines are (F) and (G) ?

8. Why are object lines made heavier than extension and dimension lines?

ASSIGNMENT A UNIT 4

Student's Name _____

1. _____

2. _____

3. _____

4. _____

5. _____

6. _____

7. _____

8. _____

_____

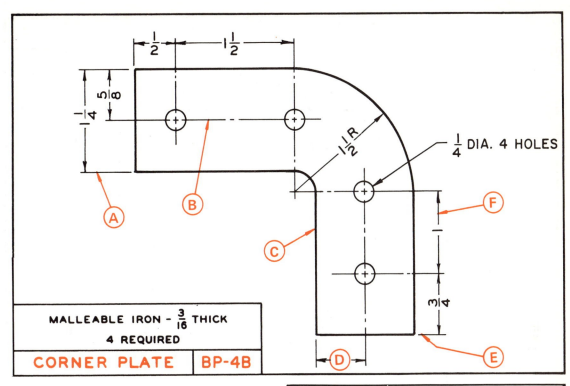

MALLEABLE IRON – $\frac{3}{16}$ THICK
4 REQUIRED

CORNER PLATE | **BP-4B**

CORNER PLATE (BP-4B)

1. What kind of line is (A) ?

2. What kind of line is (B) ?

3. What kind of line is (C) ?

4. Determine the overall length of the Plate from left to right.

5. Determine the overall width of the Plate from top to bottom.

6. Give the center distance between the two upper holes.

7. Determine distance (D) .

8. What kind of line is (E) ?

9. What kind of line is (F) ?

10. What radius forms the rounded corner of the Plate?

11. Name the material specified for the Plate.

12. How many Corner Plates are required?

ASSIGNMENT B   UNIT 4

Student's Name _____

1. _____

2. _____

3. _____

4. _____

5. _____

6. _____

7. _____

8. _____

9. _____

10. _____

11. _____

12. _____

UNIT 5 *PROJECTION LINES, OTHER LINES, LINE COMBINATIONS*

PROJECTION LINES

Projection lines are used by draftspersons and designers to establish the relationship of lines and surfaces in one view with corresponding points in other views. Projection lines, figure 5-1, are fine, unbroken lines projected from a point in one view to locate the same point in another view. Projection lines do not appear on finished drawings except where a part is complicated and it becomes necessary to show how certain details on a drawing are obtained.

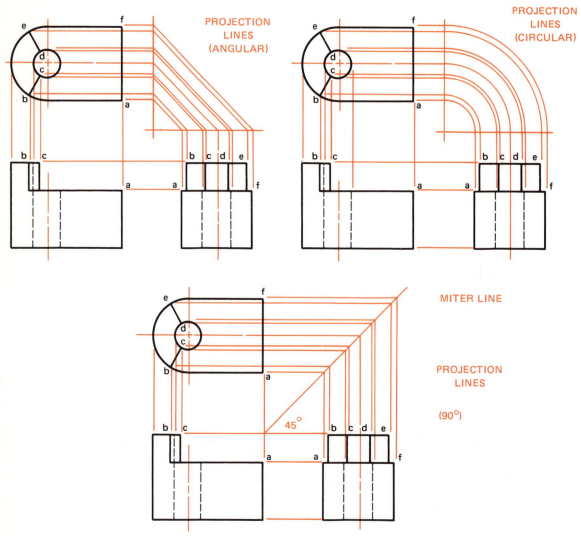

FIGURE 5-1 APPLICATION OF PROJECTION LINES

OTHER LINES

In addition to the six common types of lines, the alphabet of lines also includes other types such as the cutting plane line, break lines, lines to indicate adjacent parts and alternate positions, and lines for repeated detail. These less frequently used lines, figure 5-2, are found in more advanced drawings, and will be described in greater detail as they are used in later drawings in this text.

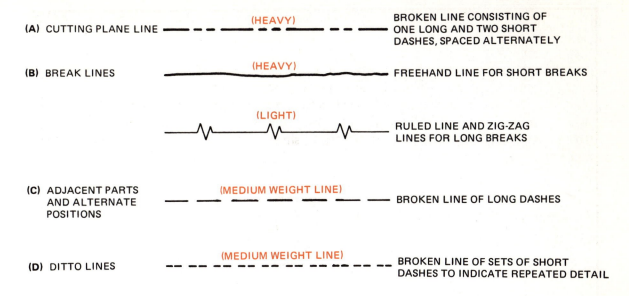

(A) CUTTING PLANE LINE — (HEAVY) — BROKEN LINE CONSISTING OF ONE LONG AND TWO SHORT DASHES, SPACED ALTERNATELY

(B) BREAK LINES — (HEAVY) — FREEHAND LINE FOR SHORT BREAKS

(LIGHT) — RULED LINE AND ZIG-ZAG LINES FOR LONG BREAKS

(C) ADJACENT PARTS AND ALTERNATE POSITIONS — (MEDIUM WEIGHT LINE) — BROKEN LINE OF LONG DASHES

(D) DITTO LINES — (MEDIUM WEIGHT LINE) — BROKEN LINE OF SETS OF SHORT DASHES TO INDICATE REPEATED DETAIL

FIGURE 5-2 SAMPLES OF OTHER LINES USED ON DRAWINGS

LINES USED IN COMBINATION

Most drawings consist of a series of object lines, hidden lines, center lines, extension lines, and dimension lines used in combination with each other to give a full description of a part or mechanism, figure 5-3.

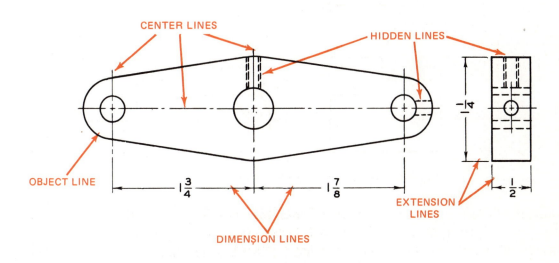

FIGURE 5-3 LINES USED IN COMBINATION

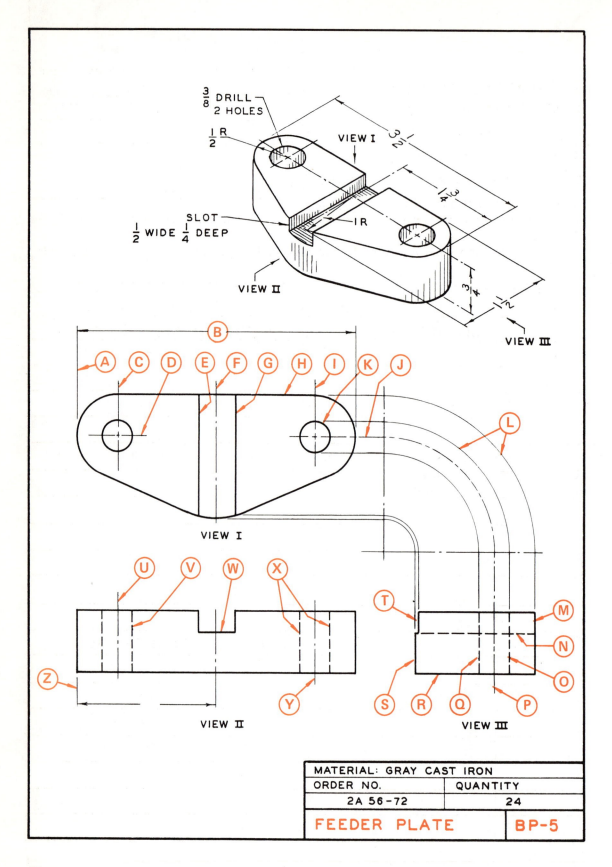

$\frac{3}{8}$ DRILL 2 HOLES

$\frac{1}{2}$ R

VIEW I

$3\frac{1}{2}$

$3\frac{1}{4}$

SLOT

$\frac{1}{2}$ WIDE $\frac{1}{4}$ DEEP

I R

VIEW II

$\frac{3}{4}$

$\frac{1}{2}$

VIEW III

VIEW I

VIEW II

VIEW III

MATERIAL: GRAY CAST IRON	
ORDER NO.	QUANTITY
2A 56-72	24
FEEDER PLATE	BP-5

16

FEEDER PLATE (BP-5)

1. What is the name of the part?

2. What is the blueprint number?

3. What is the Plate order number?

4. How many parts are to be made?

5. Name the material specified for the part.

ASSIGNMENT UNIT 5

Student's Name _____

1. _____

2. _____

3. _____

4. _____

5. _____

6. Study the Feeder Plate, BP-5.
   a. Locate and name each line from (A) to (Z) in the space provided for each in the table.
   b. Tell how each line from (A) to (L) is identified. (NOTE: Line (A) is filled in as a guide.)

LINE OF DRAWING	(A) NAME OF LINE	(B) HOW THE LINE IS IDENTIFIED		
(A)	EXTENSION LINE	FINE, UNBROKEN LINE		
(B)				
(C)				
(D)				
(E)				
(F)				
(G)				
(H)				
(I)				
(J)				
(K)				
(L)				
(M)		LINE	(A) NAME OF LINE	
(N)		(U)		
(O)		(V)		
(P)		(W)		
(Q)		(X)		
(R)		(Y)		
(S)		(Z)		
(T)				

UNIT **6**   *THREE-VIEW DRAWINGS*

Regularly-shaped flat objects which require only simple machining operations are often adequately described with notes on a one-view drawing (see Unit 9). However, when the shape of the object changes, portions are cut away or relieved, or complex machining or fabricating processes must be represented on a drawing, the one view may not be sufficient to describe the part accurately.

The number and selection of views is governed by the shape or complexity of the object. A view should not be drawn unless it makes a drawing easier to read or furnishes other information needed to describe the part clearly.

Throughout this text, as the student is required to interpret more complex drawings, the basic principles underlying the use of all additional views which are needed to describe the true shape of the object will be covered at that time. Immediate application of these principles will then be made on typical industrial blueprints.

The combination of front, top, and right side views represents the method most commonly used by draftspersons to describe simple objects. The manner in which each view is obtained and the interpretation of each view is discussed in this section.

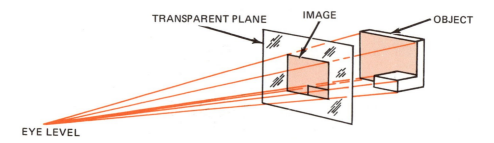

TRANSPARENT PLANE   IMAGE   OBJECT

EYE LEVEL

FIGURE 6-1 PROJECTING IMAGE FOR THE FRONT VIEW
(CONVERGING RAYS)

THE FRONT VIEW

Before an object is drawn, it is examined to determine which views will best furnish the information required to manufacture the object. The surface which is to be shown as the observer looks at the object is called the *Front View.* To draw this view, the draftsperson goes through an imaginary process of raising the object to eye level and turning it so that only one side can be seen. If an imaginary transparent plane is placed between the eye and the face of the object, parallel to the object, the image projected on the plane is the same as that formed in the eye of the observer, figure 6-1.

Note in figure 6-1 that the rays converge as they approach the observer's eye. If, instead of converging, these rays are parallel as they leave the object, the image they form on the screen is equivalent to a Front View, as shown in figure 6-2.

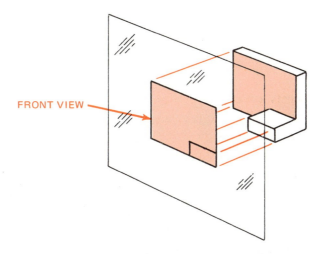

FRONT VIEW

FIGURE 6-2 FRONT VIEW OF OBJECT

THE TOP VIEW

To draw a *Top View,* the draftsperson goes through a process similar to that required to obtain the Front View. However, instead of looking squarely at the front of the object, the view is seen from a point directly above it, figure 6-3.

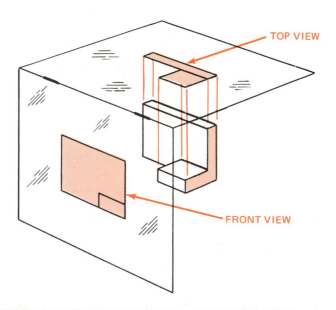

TOP VIEW

FRONT VIEW

F!GURE 6-3 PROJECTING IMAGE TO FORM THE TOP VIEW

When the horizontal plane on which the top view is projected is rotated so that it is in a vertical plane, as shown in figure 6-4, the front and top views are in their proper relationship. In other words, the top view is always placed immediately above and in line with the front view.

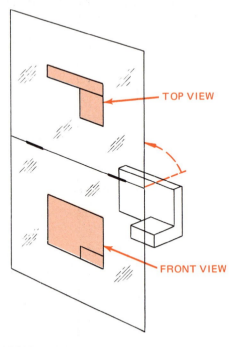

FIGURE 6-4 RELATIONSHIP OF FRONT AND TOP VIEWS

THE SIDE VIEW

A side view is developed in much the same way that the other two views were obtained. That is, the draftsperson imagines the view of the object from the side that is to be drawn. This person then proceeds to draw the object as it would appear if parallel rays were projected upon a vertical plane, figure 6-5.

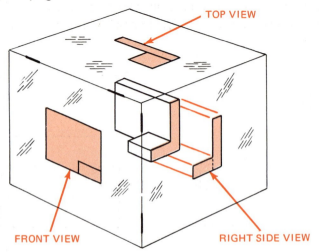

FIGURE 6-5 PROJECTING IMAGE TO FORM THE RIGHT SIDE VIEW

FRONT, TOP, AND RIGHT SIDE VIEWS

By swinging the top of the imaginary projection box to a vertical position and the right side forward, the top view is directly above the front view, and the side view is to the right of the front view and in line with it. Figure 6-6 shows the front, top, and right side views in the positions they will occupy on a blueprint.

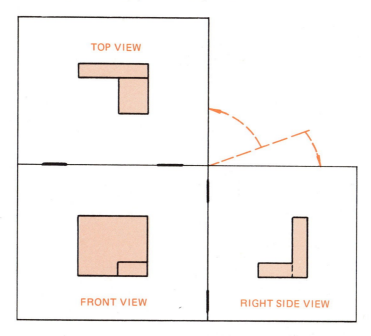

TOP VIEW

FRONT VIEW

RIGHT SIDE VIEW

FIGURE 6-6 POSITIONS OF FRONT, TOP, AND RIGHT SIDE VIEWS

WORKING DRAWINGS

An actual drawing of a part shows only the top, front, and right side views without the imaginary transparent planes, figure 6-7. These views show the exact shape and size of the object, and define the relationship of one view to another.

A mechanical drawing, when completely dimensioned and with necessary notes added, is called a *working drawing* because it furnishes all the information required to construct the object, figure 6-8.

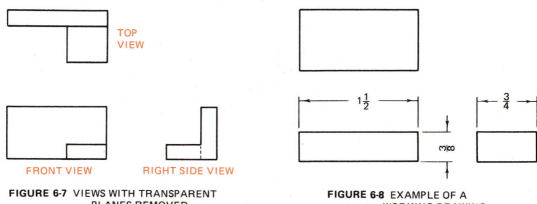

TOP VIEW

FRONT VIEW

RIGHT SIDE VIEW

FIGURE 6-7 VIEWS WITH TRANSPARENT PLANES REMOVED

FIGURE 6-8 EXAMPLE OF A WORKING DRAWING

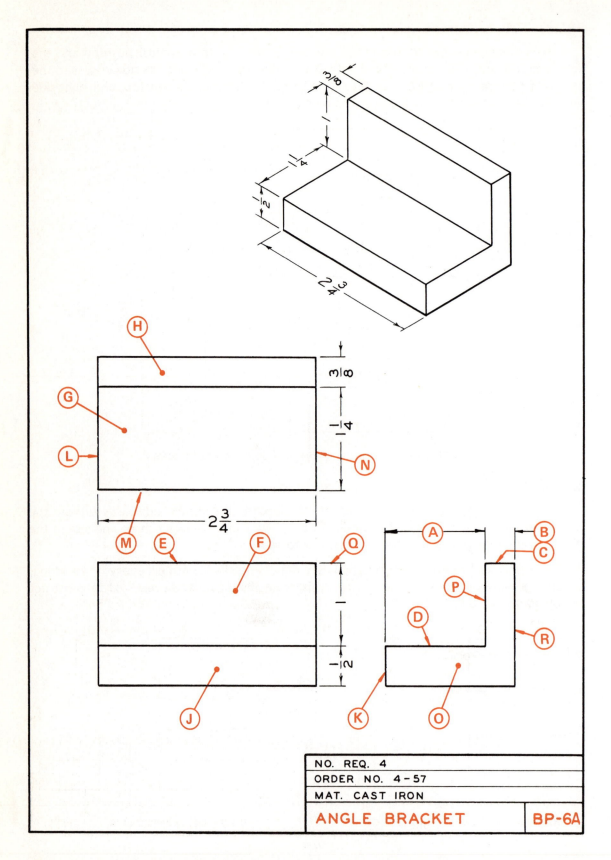

NO. REQ. 4	
ORDER NO. 4-57	
MAT. CAST IRON	
ANGLE BRACKET	BP-6A

ANGLE BRACKET (BP-6A)

1. How many Angle Brackets are required?

2. Name the material specified for the Angle Bracket.

3. State the order number of the Bracket.

4. What is the overall length of the Bracket?

5. What is the overall height?

6. What is the overall width?

7. What is dimension (A) ?

8. What is dimension (B) ?

9. What surface in the top view is represented by line (C) in the right side view?

10. Name the three views that are used to describe the shape and size of the part.

11. What surface in the top view is represented by line (D) in the right side view?

12. What line in the right side view represents surface (F) in the front view?

13. What line in the right side view represents surface (J) in the front view?

14. What line in the top view represents surface (O) in the right side view?

15. What line in the front view represents surface (H) in the top view?

16. What line in the right side view represents surface (H) in the top view?

17. What kind of lines are (E) (L) (C) (D) and (K) ?

18. What kind of lines are (A) and (B) ?

19. What encircled letter denotes an extension line?

20. What encircled letter in the front view denotes an object line?

ASSIGNMENT A   UNIT 6

Student's Name _____

1. _____

2. _____

3. _____

4. _____

5. _____

6. _____

7. _____

8. _____

9. _____

10. _____

11. _____

12. _____

13. _____

14. _____

15. _____

16. _____

17. _____

18. _____

19. _____

20. _____

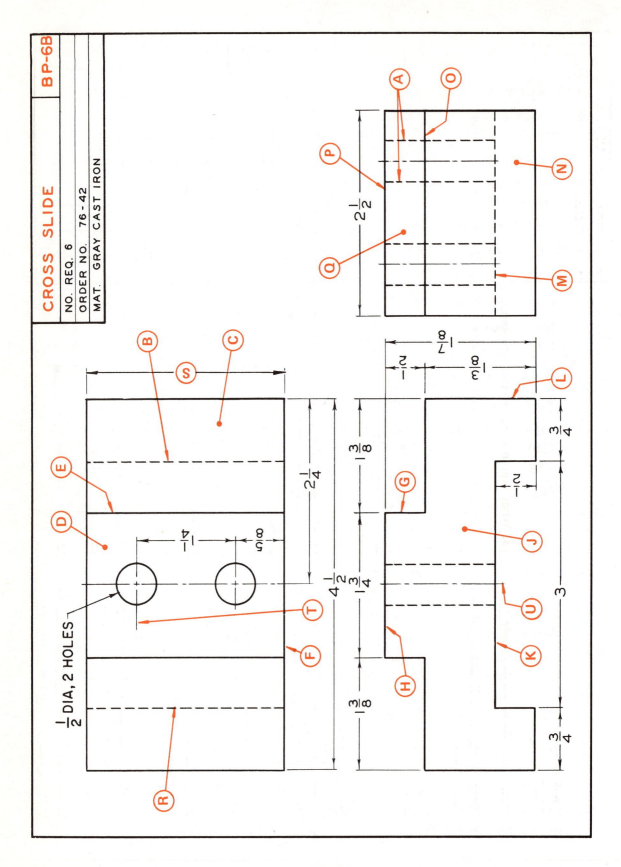

ASSIGNMENT B   UNIT 6

Student's Name _____

1. _____ 13. _____
2. _____ 14. _____
3. _____ 15. _____
4. _____ 16. _____
5. _____ 17. _____
6. _____ 18. _____
7. _____ 19. _____
8. _____ 20. _____
9. _____ 21. _____
10. _____ 22. _____
11. _____ 23. _____
12. _____ 24. _____

CROSS SLIDE (BP-6B)

1. What material is used for the Cross Slide?

2. How many pieces are required?

3. What is the overall length of the Cross Slide?

4. What is the order number?

5. What is the overall height of the Cross Slide?

6. What are the lines marked Ⓐ and Ⓑ called?

7. What do the lines marked Ⓐ represent?

8. What two lines in the top view represent the slot shown in the front view?

9. What line in the right side view represents the slot shown in the front view?

10. What line in the front view represents surface Ⓠ in the right side view?

11. What line in the front view represents surface Ⓓ in the top view?

12. What line in the top view represents surface Ⓙ in the front view?

13. What line in the side view represents surface Ⓓ in the top view?

14. What is the diameter of the holes?

15. What is the center-to-center dimension of the holes?

16. How far is the center of the first hole from the front surface of the slide?

17. Are the holes drilled all the way through the slide?

18. What is the width of the slot shown in the front view?

19. What is the depth of the slot?

20. Determine dimension Ⓢ .

21. What is the width of the projection at the top of the slide?

22. How high is the projection?

23. What kind of line is Ⓜ ?

24. What kind of line is used at Ⓞ and Ⓟ ?

25

The main purpose of a drawing is to give the technician sufficient information needed to build, inspect, or assemble a part or mechanism according to the specifications of the designer. Since the selection and arrangement of views depends upon the complexity of a part, only those views should be drawn which help in the interpretation of the drawing.

The average drawing which includes front, top, and side views is known as a three-view drawing. However, the designation of the views is not as important as the fact that the combination of views must give all the details of construction in the most understandable way.

The draftsperson usually selects as a front view of the object that view which best describes the general shape of the part. This front view may have no relationship to the actual front position of the part as it fits into a mechanism.

The names and positions of the different views that may be used to describe an object are illustrated in figure 7-1. Note that the back view may be placed in any one of three locations. The views which are easiest to read and, at the same time, furnish all the required information, should be the views selected for the drawing.

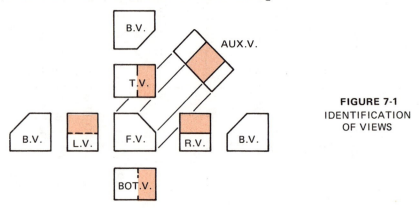

FIGURE 7-1
IDENTIFICATION
OF VIEWS

The name and abbreviation for each view is identified throughout this text as shown in figure 7-2.

NAME OF VIEW	ABBREVIATION
Front View	(F.V.)
Right Side View	(R.V.)
Left Side View	(L.V.)
Bottom View	(Bot. V.)
Back or Rear View	(B.V.)
Auxiliary View	(Aux. V.)
Top View	(T.V.)

FIGURE 7-2 ABBREVIATION OF VIEWS

ASSIGNMENT

PEDESTAL (BP-7)

Student's Name _____

Place the names of the views in the spaces provided in figures 7-3, 7-4, and 7-5.

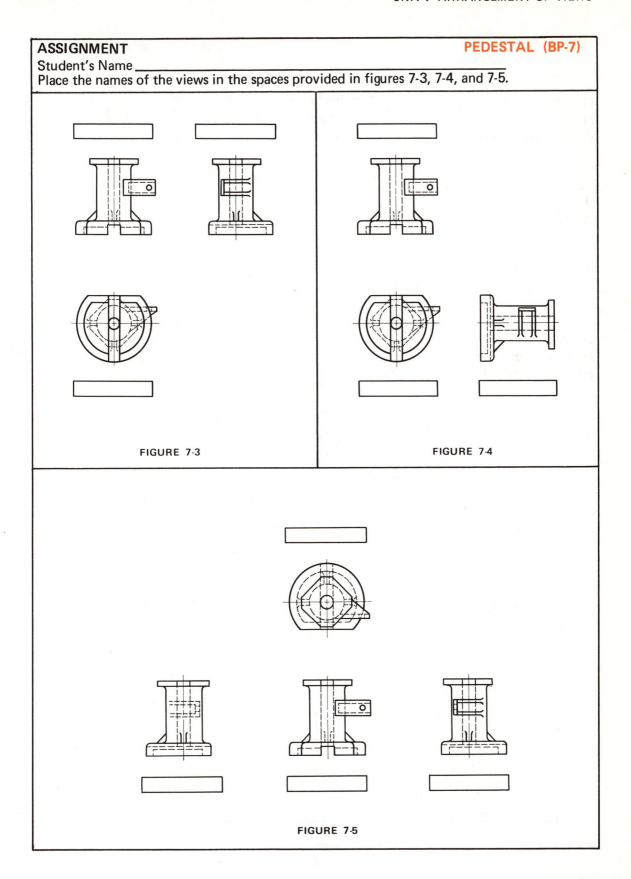

FIGURE 7-3

FIGURE 7-4

FIGURE 7-5

Simple, symmetrical flat objects and cylindrical parts, such as sleeves, shafts, rods, and studs, require only two views to give the full details of construction, figure 8-1. The two views usually include the front view and a right-side or left-side view, or a top or bottom view.

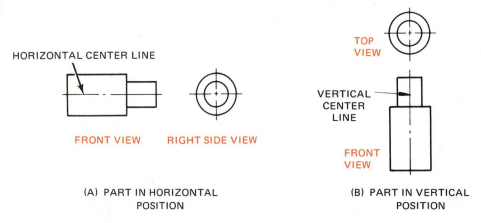

FIGURE 8-1 EXAMPLES OF TWO-VIEW DRAWINGS OF A PLUG

In the front view, figure 8-1, the center line runs through the axis of the part as a horizontal center line. If the plug is in a vertical position, the center line runs through the axis as a vertical center line.

The second view of the two-view drawing contains a horizontal and a vertical center line intersecting at the center of the circles which make up the part in this view.

The selection of views for a two-view drawing rests largely with the draftsperson or designer. Some of the combinations of views commonly used in industrial blueprints are shown in figure 8-2.

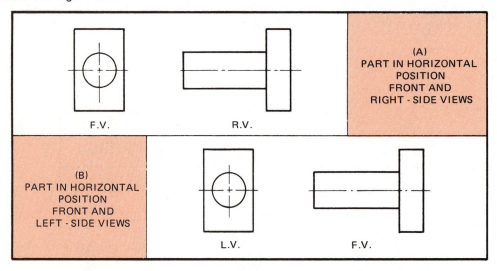

FIGURE 8-2 COMBINATION OF VIEWS FOR A TWO-VIEW DRAWING OF A PIN

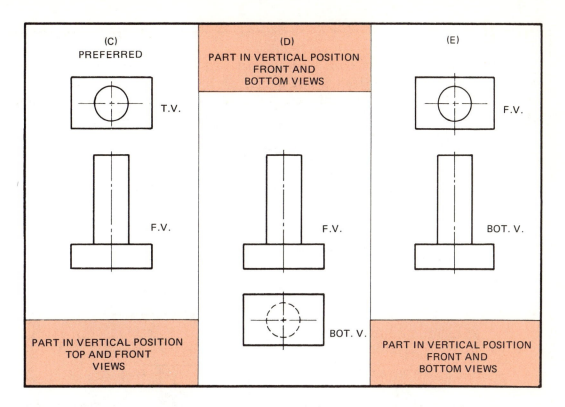

FIGURE 8-2 (CONT'D) COMBINATION OF VIEWS FOR A TWO-VIEW DRAWING OF A PIN

Note in figures 8-2 (A), (B), (C), (D), and (E) that different names are used to identify the same views. The name of each view depends on how the draftsperson views the object to obtain the front view.

REPRESENTING INVISIBLE CIRCLES

A hidden detail may be straight, curved, or cylindrical. Whatever the shape of the detail, and regardless of the number or positions of views, the hidden detail is represented by a hidden edge or invisible edge line, figure 8-3.

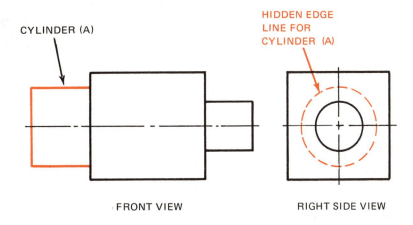

FIGURE 8-3 USE OF INVISIBLE EDGE LINES

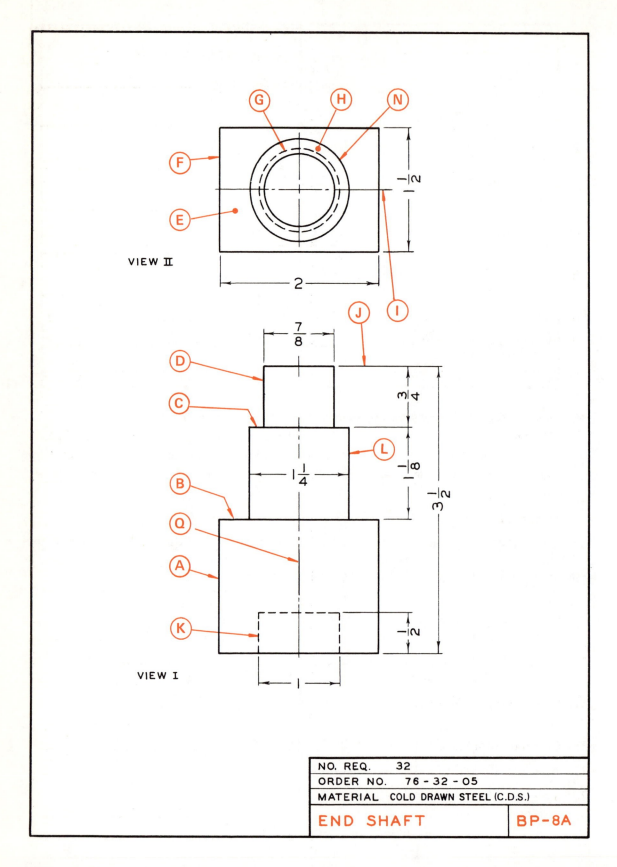

VIEW II

VIEW I

NO. REQ.	32	
ORDER NO.	76 - 32 - 05	
MATERIAL	COLD DRAWN STEEL (C.D.S.)	
END SHAFT		BP-8A

END SHAFT (BP-8A)

1. Name the two views shown.

2. What line in View II represents surface (A)?

3. What lettered surface in View II represents surface (B)?

4. What circle in View II represents the 1'' hole?

5. What line in View I represents surface (H)?

6. Name line (I).

7. What kind of line is (D)?

8. Name line (J).

9. What kind of line is (K)?

10. What circle in the top view represents diameter (L)?

11. What letters in View I represent object lines?

12. What letters in Views I and II represent center lines?

13. Give the diameter of (L).

14. What is the smallest diameter of the shaft?

15. Determine the length of the 1 1/4'' diameter portion.

16. What is the length of the rectangular part of the shaft?

17. Give the dimensions of the rectangular part.

18. Give the overall length of the shaft.

19. What is the order number?

20. State the material from which the shaft is to be machined.

ASSIGNMENT A   UNIT 8

Student's Name _____

1. _____
2. _____
3. _____
4. _____
5. _____
6. _____
7. _____
8. _____
9. _____
10. _____
11. _____
12. _____
13. _____
14. _____
15. _____
16. _____
17. _____
18. _____
19. _____
20. _____

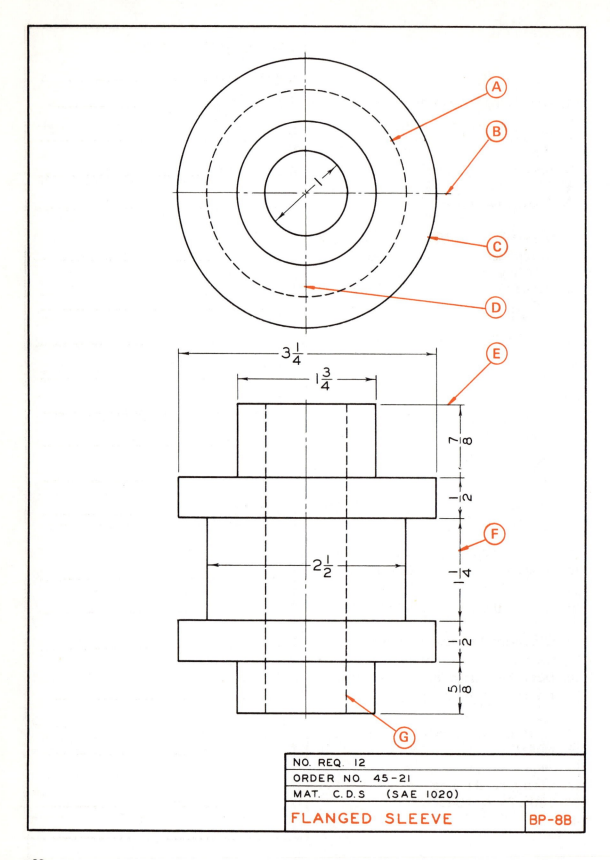

NO. REQ. 12

ORDER NO. 45-21

MAT. C.D.S   (SAE 1020)

FLANGED SLEEVE   BP-8B

FLANGED SLEEVE (BP-8B)

1. What is the name of the part?

2. What is the order number?

3. How many pieces are required?

4. What material is used?

5. Name the two views which are used to represent the Flanged Sleeve.

6. Name the kind of line indicated by each of the following encircled letters.

(A)

(B)

(C)

(D)

(E)

(F)

(G)

7. What is the outside diameter of both flanges?

8. What is the thickness of each flange?

9. What is the diameter of the center hole?

10. Does the hole go all the way through the center of the sleeve?

11. What is the diameter of the hidden circle?

12. Determine the total or overall length of the Flanged Sleeve.

ASSIGNMENT B   UNIT 8

Student's Name _____

1. _____

2. _____

3. _____

4. _____

5. _____

6.
(A) _____

(B) _____

(C) _____

(D) _____

(E) _____

(F) _____

(G) _____

7. _____

8. _____

9. _____

10. _____

11. _____

12. _____

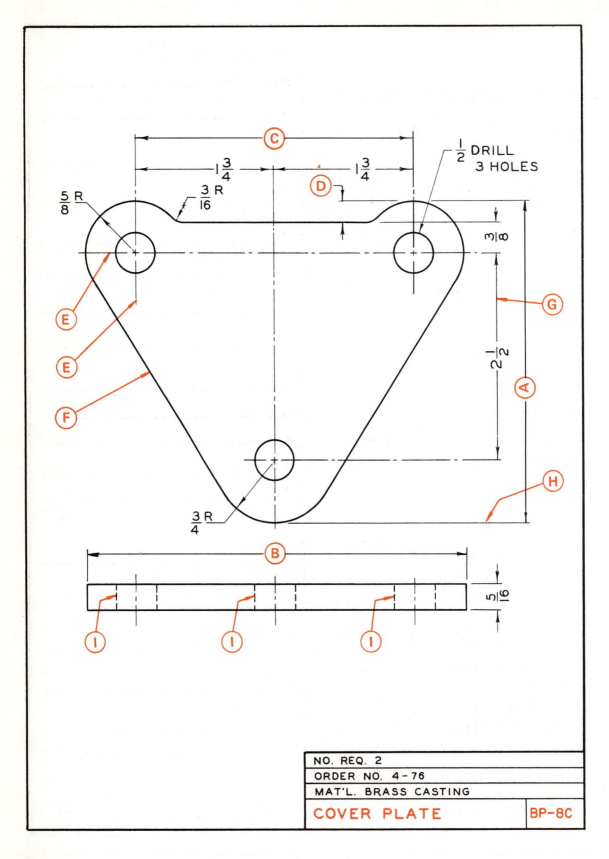

$\frac{1}{2}$ DRILL
3 HOLES

NO. REQ. 2

ORDER NO. 4-76

MAT'L. BRASS CASTING

COVER PLATE   BP-8C

COVER PLATE (BP-8C)

1. Name the material specified for the part.

2. Name the two views used to describe the part.

3. Identify the kind of line indicated by each of the following encircled letters.

    (E)

    (F)

    (G)

    (H)

    (I)

4. What is the overall width (A) ?

5. What is the overall length (B) ?

6. How many holes are to be drilled?

7. What is the thickness of the plate?

8. What is the diameter of the holes?

9. What is the distance between the center of one of the two upper holes and the center line of the Plate?

10. Give the center distance (C) of the two upper holes?

11. What is the radius that forms the two upper rounds of the Plate?

12. What radius forms the lower part of the Plate?

13. What kind of line is drawn through the center of the Plate?

14. Determine distance (D) .

15. How much stock is left between the edge of one of the upper holes and the outside of the piece?

ASSIGNMENT C   UNIT 8

Student's Name _____

1. _____

2. _____

3.
(E) _____
(F) _____
(G) _____
(H) _____
(I) _____

4. _____

5. _____

6. _____

7. _____

8. _____

9. _____

10. _____

11. _____

12. _____

13. _____

14. _____

15. _____

UNIT 9 — ONE-VIEW DRAWINGS

Many parts which are uniform in shape require only one view to describe them adequately. This is particularly true of cylindrical objects where a one-view drawing saves drafting time and simplifies the reading of the blueprint.

When a one-view drawing of a cylinder is used, the dimensions showing the diameter must be followed by the letters *DIA* or *D* as shown in figure 9-1. This abbreviation of DIA for diameter and the use of a center line indicate that the part is cylindrical.

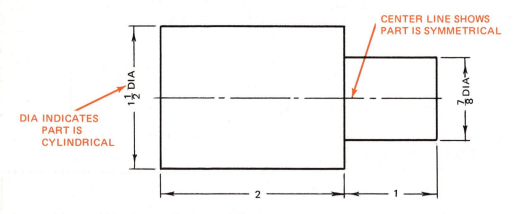

FIGURE 9-1 ONE-VIEW DRAWING OF A CYLINDRICAL SHAFT

The one-view drawing is also used extensively for flat parts. With the addition of notes to supplement the dimensions on the view, the one view furnishes all the necessary information for accurately describing the part, figure 9-2.

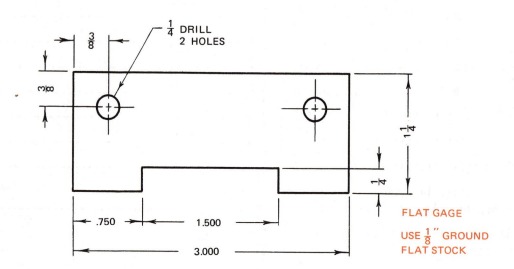

FIGURE 9-2 ONE-VIEW DRAWING OF A FLAT PART

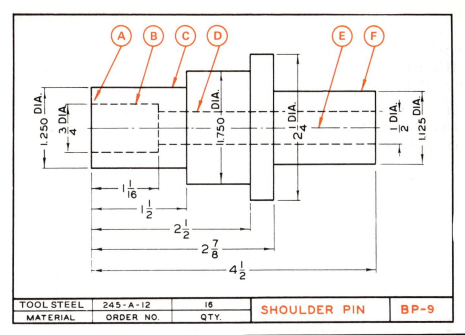

TOOL STEEL	245-A-12	16	SHOULDER PIN	BP-9
MATERIAL	ORDER NO.	QTY.		

SHOULDER PIN (BP-9)

1. Name the view represented on BP-9.

2. What is the shape of the Shoulder Pin?

3. How many outside diameters are shown?

4. What is the largest diameter?

5. What diameter is the smallest hole?

6. What is the overall length of the pin?

7. How deep is the 3/4" hole?

8. How wide is the 1.750" DIA portion?

9. What letters represent object lines?

10. What kinds of lines are Ⓑ and Ⓓ ?

11. What letter represents the center line?

12. What does the center line indicate about the holes and outside diameters?

13. Give the width of the 2 1/4" DIA portion.

14. State the order number of the part.

15. What is the material specified for the pins?

ASSIGNMENT   UNIT 9

Student's Name _____

1. _____
2. _____
3. _____
4. _____
5. _____
6. _____
7. _____
8. _____
9. _____
10. _____
11. _____
12. _____
13. _____
14. _____
15. _____

As long as all the surfaces of an object are parallel or at right angles to one another, they may be represented in one or more regular views, figure 10-1.

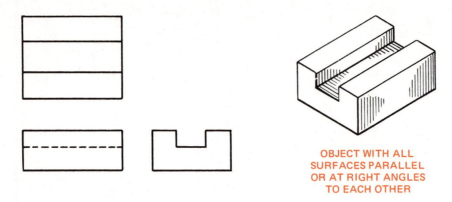

OBJECT WITH ALL
SURFACES PARALLEL
OR AT RIGHT ANGLES
TO EACH OTHER

FIGURE 10-1 REPRESENTATION OF OBJECT USING REGULAR VIEWS

The surfaces of such objects can be projected in their true sizes and shapes on either a horizontal or a vertical plane, or on any combination of these planes.

Some objects have one or more surfaces which slant and are inclined away from either a horizontal or vertical plane. In this situation the regular views will not show the true shape of the inclined surface, figure 10-2. If the true shape must be shown, the drawing must include an *auxiliary view* to represent the angular surface accurately. The auxiliary view is in addition to the regular views.

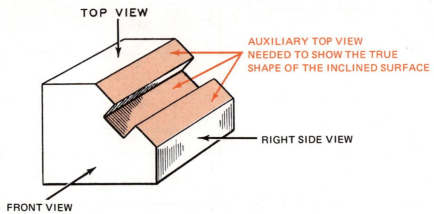

TOP VIEW

AUXILIARY TOP VIEW
NEEDED TO SHOW THE TRUE
SHAPE OF THE INCLINED SURFACE

RIGHT SIDE VIEW

FRONT VIEW

FIGURE 10-2 OBJECT REQUIRING USE OF AUXILIARY VIEW

APPLICATION OF AUXILIARY VIEWS

Auxiliary views may be full views or partial views. Figure 10-3 shows an auxiliary view in which only the inclined surface and other required details are included. In an auxiliary view, the inclined surface is projected on an imaginary plane which is parallel to it. Rounded surfaces and circular holes, which are distorted and appear as ellipses in the regular views, will appear in their true shapes and sizes in an auxiliary view.

Auxiliary views are named according to the position from which the inclined face is seen. For example, the auxiliary view may be an auxiliary front, top, bottom, left side, or right side view. On drawings of complex parts involving compound angles, one auxiliary view may be developed from another auxiliary view. The first auxiliary view is called the *primary* view, and those views developed from it are called *secondary* auxiliary views. For the present, attention is focused on primary auxiliary views.

SUMMARY

Auxiliary views are usually partial views which show only the inclined surface of an object. In figure 10-3, the true size and shape of surface (A) is shown in the auxiliary view of the angular surface.

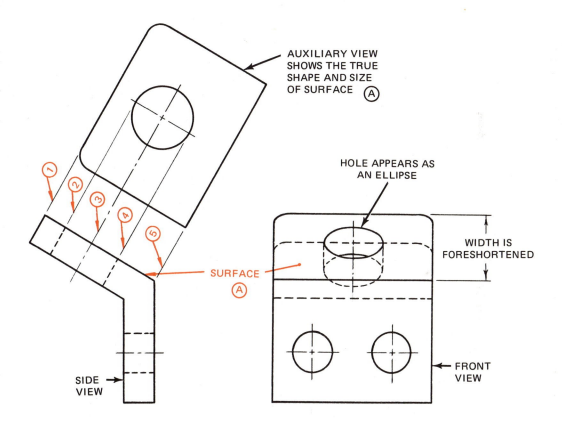

FIGURE 10-3 APPLICATION OF AN AUXILIARY VIEW

The draftsperson develops this view by projecting lines (1), (2), (3), (4) and (5) at right angles to surface (A). When the front view is compared with the auxiliary partial view, it can be seen that the hole in surface (A) appears as an ellipse in the front view. The width of surface (A) is foreshortened in the regular view while the true shape and size are shown on the auxiliary view.

In figure 10-3, the combination of *left side view, auxiliary partial top view* and *front view,* when properly dimensioned, shows all surfaces in their true size and shape. As a result, these are the only views required to describe this part completely.

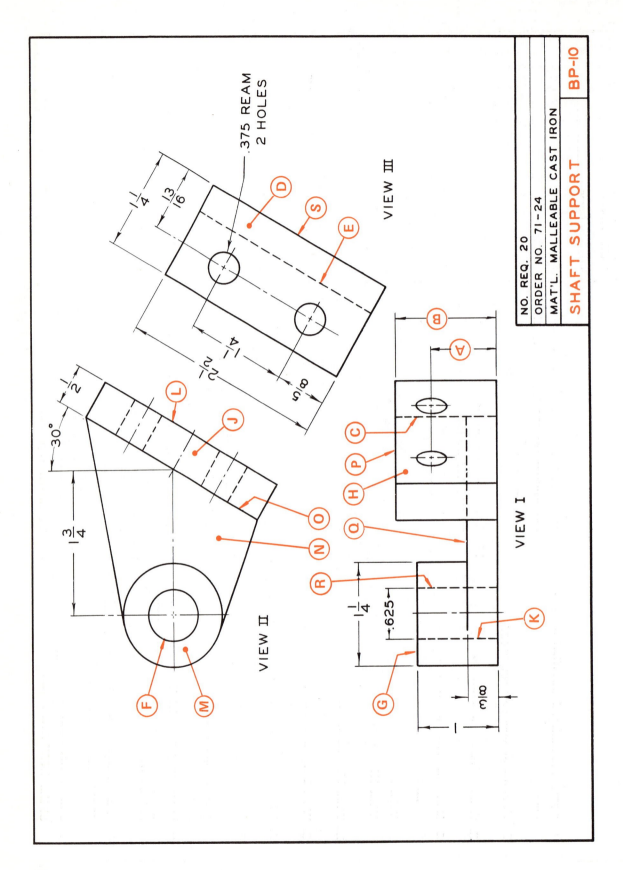

.375 REAM
2 HOLES

VIEW III

VIEW I

VIEW II

NO. REQ. 20
ORDER NO. 71-24
MAT'L. MALLEABLE CAST IRON
SHAFT SUPPORT   BP-10

ASSIGNMENT UNIT 10

Student's Name _____

1. _____
2. _____
3. _____
4. (I) _____
   (II) _____
   (III) _____
5. _____
6. _____
7. _____
8. _____
9. _____
10. _____
11. _____
12. _____
13. _____
14. _____
15. _____
16. _____
17. _____
18. _____
19. _____
20. _____

SHAFT SUPPORT (BP-10)

1. Name the material specified for the part.

2. How many pieces are required?

3. What is the order number?

4. Name each of the following:
   View I
   View II
   View III

5. What kind of line is Ⓒ ?

6. What kind of line is Ⓟ ?

7. Give the diameter of **hole** Ⓕ .

8. Determine dimension Ⓐ .

9. Determine dimension Ⓑ .

10. What surface in the front view is the same as surface Ⓓ in the auxiliary view?

11. How many .375″ DIA holes must be reamed in the support?

12. What is the center-to-center distance of the .375″ DIA holes?

13. What surface in the top view is represented by the line Ⓔ in the auxiliary view?

14. What surface in the top view is represented by line Ⓖ in the front view?

15. What line in the top view represents surface Ⓗ in the front view?

16. What line in the front view represents surface Ⓙ in the top view?

17. What do lines Ⓚ and Ⓡ represent?

18. What line in the front view represents surface Ⓝ in the top view?

19. Determine the vertical distance between the surface represented by the line Ⓟ and the surface represented by line Ⓠ .

20. What is the distance between the surface represented by line Ⓔ and the surface represented by line Ⓢ ?

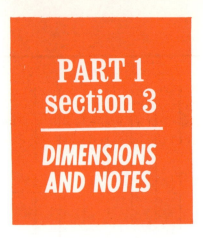

UNIT 11 — CONSTRUCTION, SIZE, LOCATION DIMENSIONS

Drawings consist of several types of lines which are used singly or in combination with each other to describe the shape and internal construction of an object or mechanism. However, to construct or machine a part, the blueprint or drawing must include dimensions which indicate exact sizes and locations of surfaces, indentations, holes, and other details.

The lines and dimensions, in turn, are supplemented by notes which give additional information. This information includes the kind of material used, the degree of machining accuracy required, details regarding the assembly of parts, and any other data which the craftsperson needs to know to make and assemble the part.

THE LANGUAGE OF DRAFTING

To insure some measure of uniformity in industrial drawings, the American National Standards Institute (ANSI) has established drafting standards. These standards are called the language of drafting and are in general use throughout the United States. While these drafting standards or practices may vary in some respects between industries, the principles are basically the same. The practices recommended by ANSI for dimensioning and for making notes are followed in this section.

Standards for Dimensioning

All drawings should be dimensioned completely so that a minimum of computation is necessary, and the parts can be built without scaling the drawing. However, there should not be a duplication of dimensions unless such dimensions make the drawing clearer and easier to read.

Many parts cannot be drawn full size because they are too large to fit a standard drawing sheet, or too small to have all details shown clearly. The draftsperson can, however, still represent such objects either by reducing (in the case of large objects) or enlarging (for small objects) the size to which the drawing is made.

This practice does not affect any dimensions as the dimensions on a drawing give the actual sizes. If a drawing 6″ long represents a part 12″ long, a note should appear in the title box of the drawing to indicate the *scale* that is used. This scale is the ratio of the drawing size to the actual size of the object. In this case, the scale 6″ = 12″ is called *half scale* or 1/2″ = 1″. Other common scales include the one-quarter scale (1/4″ = 1″), one-eighth scale (1/8″ = 1″), and the double size scale (2″ = 1″).

CONTRUCTION DIMENSIONS

Dimensions used in building a part are sometimes called *construction dimensions.* These dimensions serve two purposes: (1) they indicate size, and (2) they give exact locations. For example, to drill a through hole in a part, the technician must know the diameter of the hole, and the exact location of the center of the hole, figure 11-1.

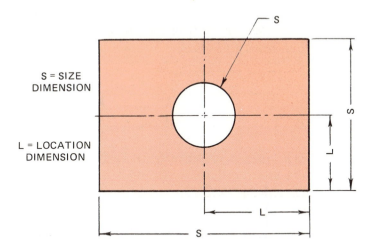

FIGURE 11-1 DIMENSIONS INDICATING SIZE AND LOCATION

SIZE DIMENSIONS

Every solid has three size dimensions: length, width, and thickness. In the case of a regular prism, two of the dimensions are usually placed on the principal view and the third dimension is placed on one of the other views, figure 11-2.

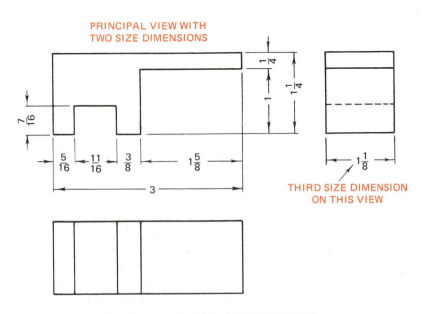

FIGURE 11-2 PLACING SIZE DIMENSIONS

LOCATION DIMENSIONS

Location dimensions are usually made from either a center line or a finished surface. This practice is followed to overcome inaccuracies due to variations in measurement caused by surface irregularities.

Draftspersons and designers must know all the manufacturing processes and operations which a part must undergo in the shop. This technical information assists them in placing size and location dimensions, required for each operation, on the drawing. Figure 11-3 shows how size and location dimensions are indicated.

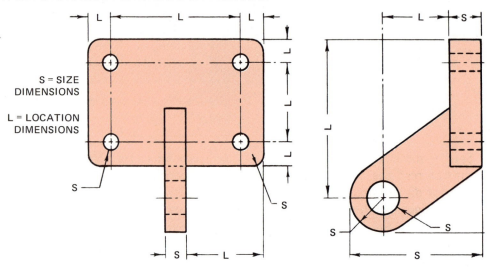

S = SIZE
DIMENSIONS

L = LOCATION
DIMENSIONS

FIGURE 11-3 SIZE AND LOCATION DIMENSIONS

PLACING DIMENSIONS

In dimensioning a drawing, the first step is to place extension lines and external center lines where needed, figure 11-4.

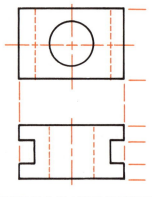

FIGURE 11-4 PLACING EXTENSION
LINES AND CENTER LINES

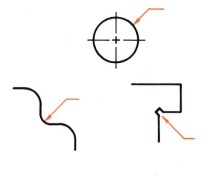

FIGURE 11-5 LEADERS USED
FOR DIMENSIONING

Dimension lines and leaders are added next. The term *leader* refers to a light straight line terminating in an arrowhead. The leader directs attention to a dimension and the arrowhead identifies the surface to which the dimension refers. A few sample leaders are given in figure 11-5.

The common practice in placing dimensions is to keep them outside the outline of the object. The exception is where the drawing may be made clearer by inserting the dimensions within the object. When a dimension applies to two views, it should be placed between the two views as shown in figure 11-6.

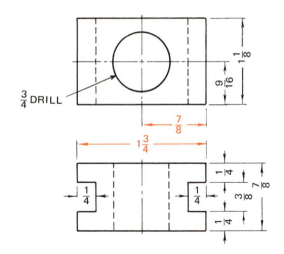

FIGURE 11-6 PLACING DIMENSIONS BETWEEN VIEWS

Continuous Dimensions

Sets of dimension lines and numerals should be placed on drawings close enough so they may be read easily without any possibility of confusing one dimension with another. If a series of dimensions is required, the dimensions should be placed in a line as continuous dimensions, figure 11-7A. This method is preferred over the staggering of dimensions, figure 11-7B, because of ease in reading, appearance, and simplified dimensioning.

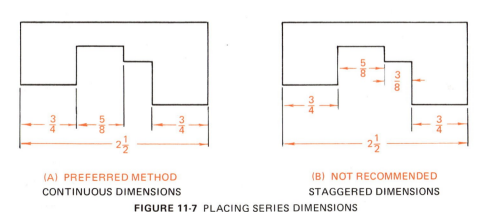

(A) PREFERRED METHOD
CONTINUOUS DIMENSIONS

(B) NOT RECOMMENDED
STAGGERED DIMENSIONS

FIGURE 11-7 PLACING SERIES DIMENSIONS

DIMENSIONS IN LIMITED SPACES

In the dimensioning of grooves or slots, the dimension, in many cases, extends beyond the width of the extension line. In such instances, the dimension is placed on either side of the extension line, or a leader is used, figure 11-8.

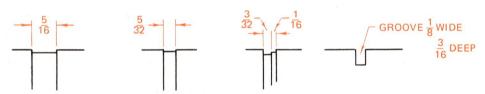

FIGURE 11-8 DIMENSIONING GROOVES AND SLOTS IN LIMITED SPACES

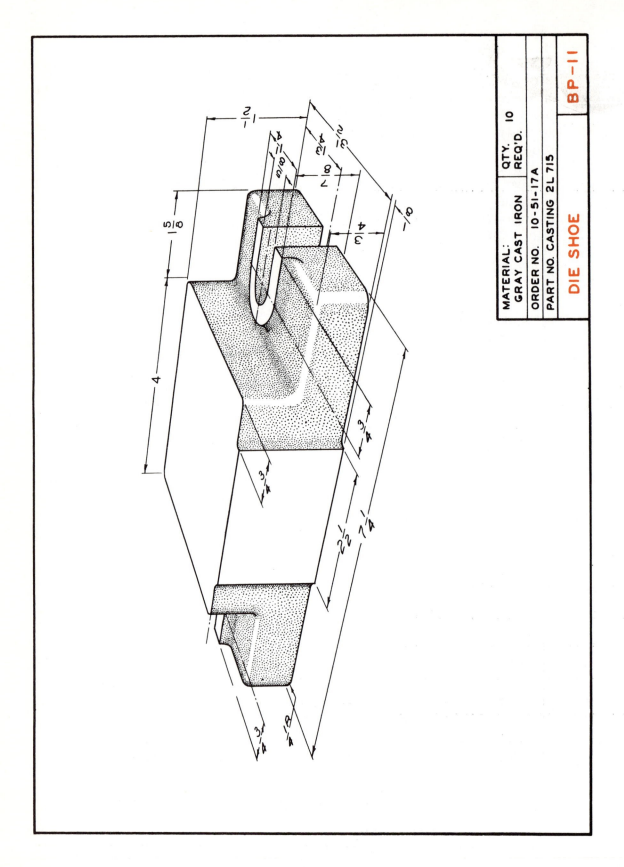

MATERIAL:
GRAY CAST IRON

QTY.
REQ'D. 10

ORDER NO. 10-51-17A

PART NO. CASTING 2L 715

DIE SHOE

BP-11

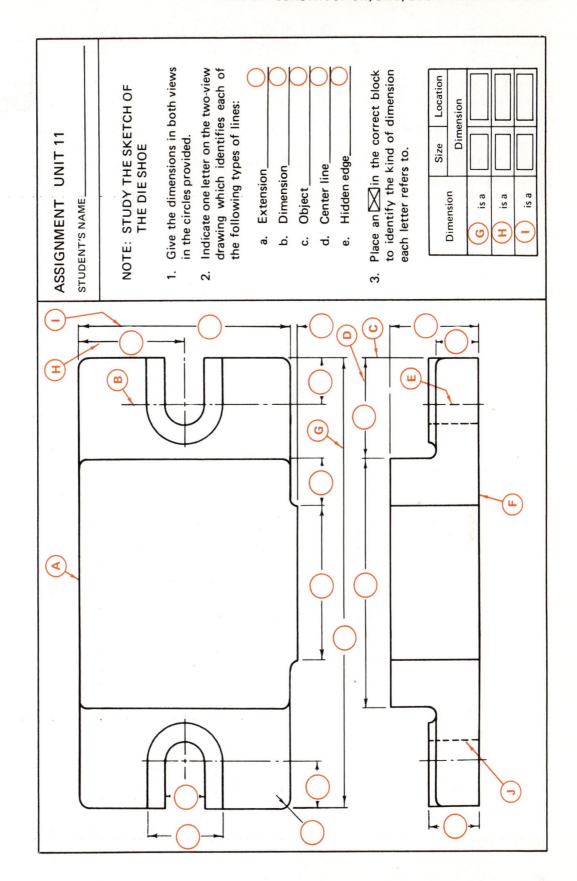

ASSIGNMENT UNIT 11

STUDENT'S NAME:

NOTE: STUDY THE SKETCH OF
       THE DIE SHOE

1. Give the dimensions in both views
    in the circles provided.

2. Indicate one letter on the two-view
    drawing which identifies each of
    the following types of lines:

    a. Extension

    b. Dimension

    c. Object

    d. Center line

    e. Hidden edge

3. Place an ☒ in the correct block
    to identify the kind of dimension
    each letter refers to.

Dimension	Size	Location
	Dimension	Dimension
G is a		
H is a		
I is a		

47

UNIT 12 — READING DIMENSIONS; DIMENSIONING CYLINDERS, CIRCLES AND ARCS

ALIGNED AND UNIDIRECTIONAL METHODS OF PLACING AND READING DIMENSIONS

There are two standard methods of placing dimensions. In the older method, called the *aligned* method, each dimension is placed in line with the dimension to which it refers, figure 12-1A. The second method, the *unidirectional* method, has all numbers or values placed horizontally (one direction), regardless of the direction of the dimension line. All values are read from the bottom, figure 12-1B.

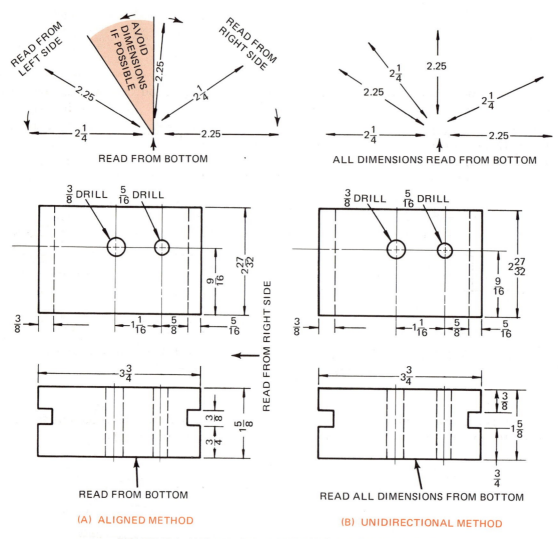

(A) ALIGNED METHOD   (B) UNIDIRECTIONAL METHOD

FIGURE 12-1 ALIGNED AND UNIDIRECTIONAL DIMENSIONING

The aligned and unidirectional methods are illustrated in figures 12-1A and 12-1B on similar drawings of the same part. Note at (A) that the aligned dimensions are read from both the bottom and the right side. By contrast, the unidirectional dimensions, figure 12-1B are read from the bottom (one direction only).

DIMENSIONING CYLINDERS

The length and diameter of a cylinder are usually placed in the view which shows the cylinder as a rectangle, figure 12-2. This method of dimensioning is preferred because on small diameter cylinders and holes a dimension placed in the hole is confusing.

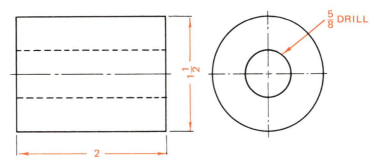

FIGURE 12-2 DIMENSIONING CYLINDERS

Many round parts, with cylindrical surfaces symmetrical about the axis, can be represented on one-view drawings. The abbreviation for diameter, DIA, is used with the dimension in such instances because no other view is needed to show the shape of the surface, figure 12-3A. On two-view drawings, DIA may be omitted, figure 12-3B. In other words, when a cylinder is dimensioned, DIA should follow the dimension unless it is evident that the dimension refers to a diameter.

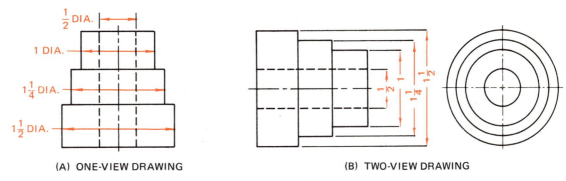

(A) ONE-VIEW DRAWING   (B) TWO-VIEW DRAWING

FIGURE 12-3 DIMENSIONING CIRCLES

DIMENSIONING ARCS

An arc is always dimensioned by giving the radius. The dimension should be followed by an 'R', and should have an arrowhead only at the outer end, figure 12-4.

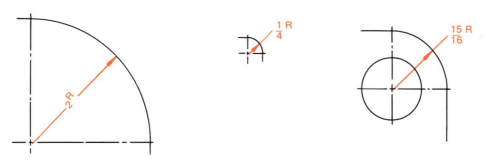

FIGURE 12-4 DIMENSIONING ARCS

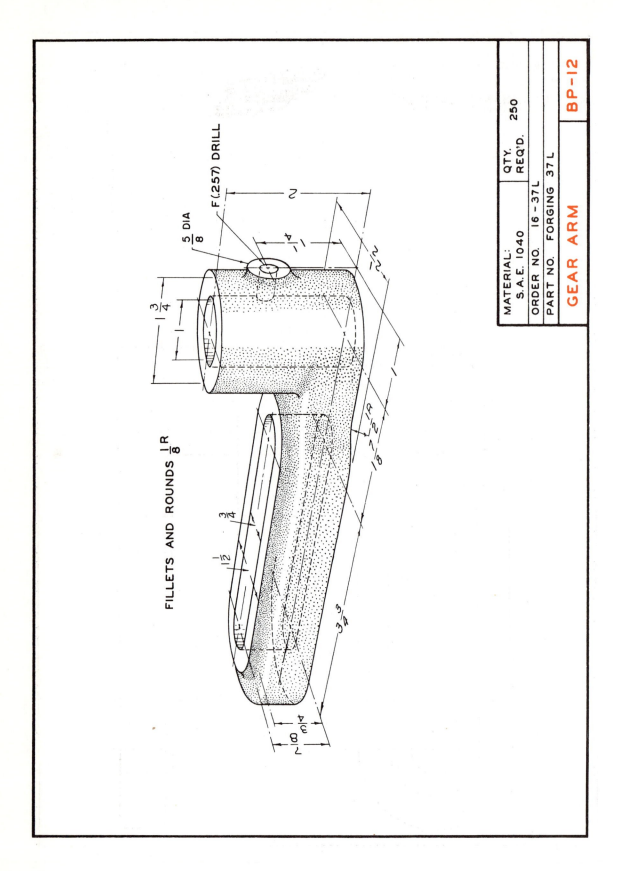

FILLETS AND ROUNDS $\frac{1}{8}$ R

$\frac{5}{8}$ DIA

F (.257) DRILL

MATERIAL: S.A.E. 1040	QTY. REQ'D.	250
ORDER NO. 16 – 37 L		
PART NO. FORGING 37 L		
GEAR ARM		BP-12

ASSIGNMENT   UNIT **12**

STUDENT'S NAME _____

NOTE: STUDY THE SKETCH OF THE GEAR ARM

1. Give the dimensions required in both views in the circles provided, using the unidirectional method.

2. Dimension arcs (A) and (B)

3. What outside diameter is the upper right portion? _____

4. Give the overall length of the elongated slot. _____

5. Determine the overall length of the Gear Arm. _____

6. Name the two views. _____ and _____ views.

7. Refer to the two-view drawing. Give one letter which identifies each type of line.
   a. Center line _____
   b. Object line _____
   c. Extension line _____
   d. Hidden edge _____
   e. Dimension line _____

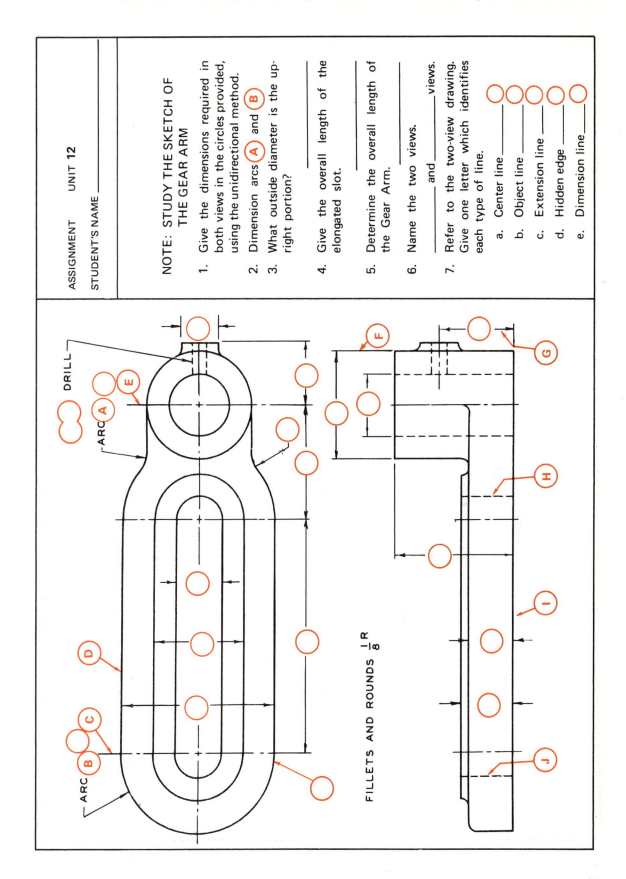

DRILL

ARC

FILLETS AND ROUNDS $\frac{1}{8}$ R

DIMENSIONING HOLES

The diameters of holes which are to be formed by drilling, reaming, or punching should have the diameter, preferably on a leader, followed by a note indicating (1) the operation to be performed, and (2) the number of holes to be produced, figure 13-1.

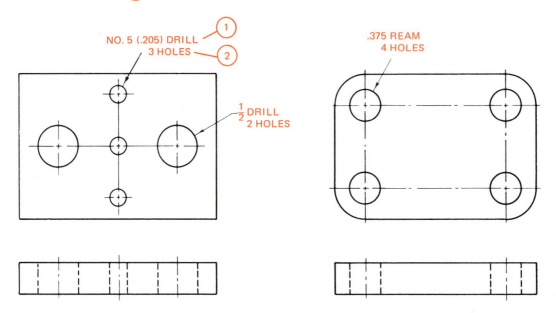

FIGURE 13-1 DIMENSIONING HOLES

DIMENSIONING COUNTERBORED HOLES

A counterbored hole, figure 13-2, is one that has been machined to a larger diameter for a specified depth so that a bolt or pin will fit into this recessed hole. The counterbored hole provides a flat surface for the bolt or pin to seat against.

Counterbored holes are dimensioned by giving (1) the diameter of the drill, (2) the diameter of the counterbore, (3) the depth, and (4) the number of holes, figure 13-2.

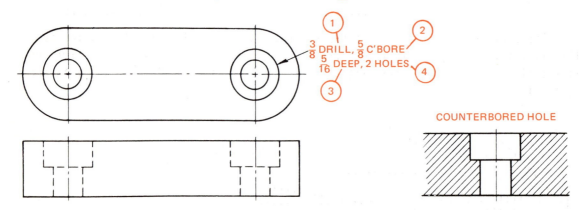

FIGURE 13-2 DIMENSIONING COUNTERBORED HOLES

DIMENSIONING COUNTERSUNK HOLES

A countersunk hole, figure 13-3 is a cone-shaped recess machined in a part to receive a cone-shaped flat head screw or bolt.

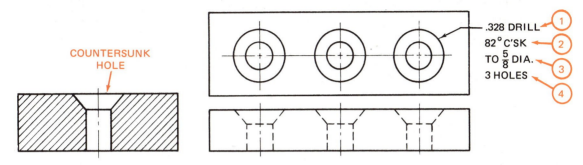

COUNTERSUNK HOLE

.328 DRILL ①
82°C'SK ②
TO $\frac{5}{8}$ DIA. ③
3 HOLES ④

FIGURE 13-3 DIMENSIONING COUNTERSUNK HOLES

Countersunk holes are dimensioned by giving ① the diameter of the hole, ② the angle at which the hole is to be countersunk, ③ the diameter at the large end of the hole, and ④ the number of holes to be countersunk.

DIMENSIONING ANGLES

The design of a part may require some lines to be drawn at an angle. The amount of the divergence (the amount the lines move away from each other) is indicated by an angle measured in degrees or fractional parts of a degree. The degree is indicated by the symbol ° placed after the numerical value of the angle. For example, in figure 13-4B, 45° indicates that the angle measures 45 degrees.

Two common methods of dimensioning angles show (1) linear dimensions or (2) angular measure as illustrated in figure 13-4A and B.

FIGURE 13-4 METHODS OF DIMENSIONING ANGLES

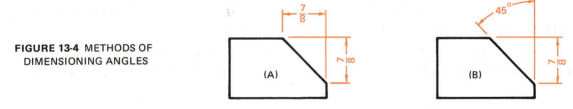

(A)

(B)

The dimension line for an angle should be an arc whose ends terminate in arrowheads. The numeral indicating the number of degrees in the angle is read in a horizontal position, except where the angle is large enough to permit the numerals to be placed along the arc, figure 13-5.

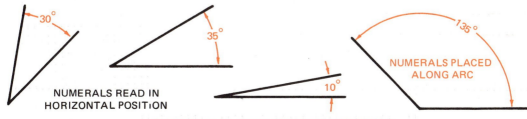

NUMERALS READ IN HORIZONTAL POSITION

NUMERALS PLACED ALONG ARC

FIGURE 13-5 PLACING ANGULAR DIMENSIONS

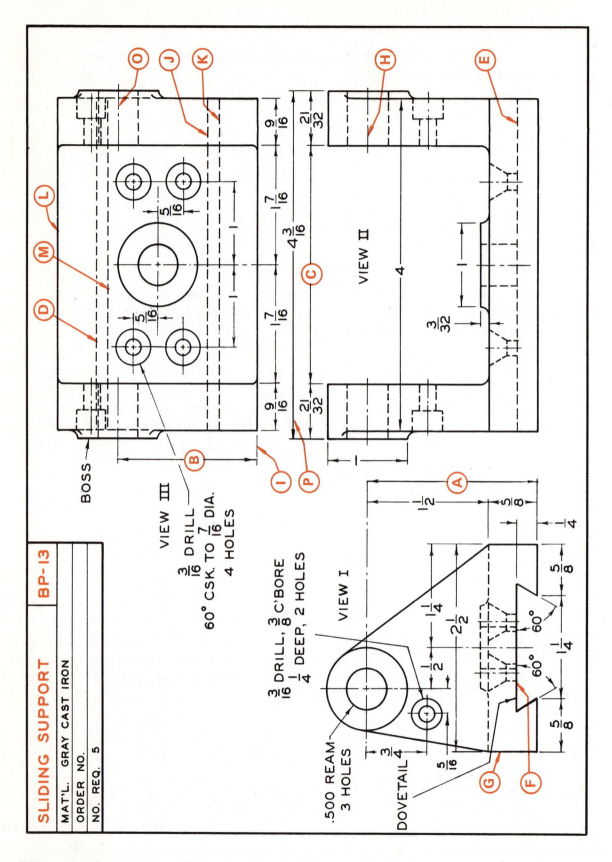

SLIDING SUPPORT | BP-13

MAT'L. GRAY CAST IRON

ORDER NO.

NO. REQ. 5

VIEW III

$\frac{3}{16}$ DRILL
60° CSK. TO $\frac{7}{16}$ DIA.
4 HOLES

BOSS

VIEW II

VIEW I

$\frac{3}{16}$ DRILL, $\frac{3}{8}$ C'BORE
$\frac{1}{4}$ DEEP, 2 HOLES

.500 REAM
3 HOLES

DOVETAIL

SLIDING SUPPORT (BP-13)

1. Name view I which shows the shape of the dovetail.

2. Name view III in which the bottom pad appears as a circle.

3. Name view II.

4. Name the kind of line shown at (E) .

5. What surface in view I is represented by line (F) ?

6. Name the kind of line shown at (G) .

7. What line in view III represents surface (G) ?

8. Name the kind of line shown at (H) .

9. What line in view III represents the line (H) ?

10. Name the kind of line shown at (I) .

11. Name the kind of line shown at (J) .

12. What lines in the top view represent the dovetail?

13. What does the line (E) in the front view represent?

14. Determine height (A) .

15. How many bosses are shown on the uprights?

16. What is the outside diameter of the boss?

17. Determine dimension (B) .

18. How far off from the center of the support is the center of the two holes in the bosses of the uprights?

19. Give the dimensions for the counter-bored holes.

20. What dimensions are given for the countersunk holes?

21. Give the dimensions of the reamed holes.

22. What is the dimension (C) ?

23. How wide is the opening in the dovetail?

24. How deep is the dovetail machined?

25. What is the angle to the horizontal at which the dovetail is cut?

ASSIGNMENT   UNIT 13

Student's Name _____

1. _____

2. _____

3. _____

4. _____

5. _____

6. _____

7. _____

8. _____

9. _____

10. _____

11. _____

12. _____

13. _____

14. _____

15. _____

16. _____

17. _____

18. _____

19. _____

20. _____

21. _____

22. _____

23. _____

24. _____

25. _____

UNIT 14 *DIMENSIONING CENTERS AND HOLES ON A CIRCLE*

DIMENSIONING A POINT OR A CENTER

A point or a center of an arc or circle is generally measured from two finished surfaces. This method of locating the center is preferred to making an angular measurement.

In figure 14-1, the center of the circle and arc may be found easily by scribing the vertical and horizontal center lines from the machined surfaces.

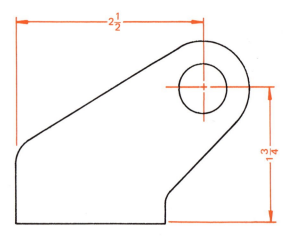

FIGURE 14-1 DIMENSIONING THE CENTER OF A CIRCLE

DIMENSIONING EQUALLY SPACED HOLES ON A CIRCLE

If a number of holes are to be equally spaced on a circle, the exact location of the first hole is given by location dimensions. To locate the remaining holes, the location dimensions are followed by ① the diameter of the holes, ② the number of holes, and ③ the notation "equally spaced", figure 14-2.

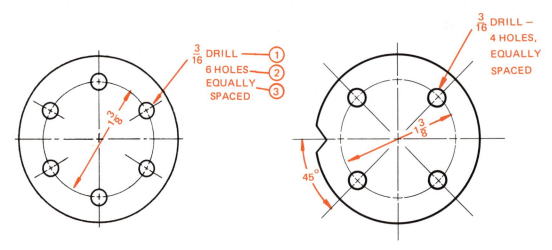

FIGURE 14-2 DIMENSIONING HOLES EQUALLY SPACED ON A CIRCLE

DIMENSIONING UNEQUALLY SPACED HOLES ON A CIRCLE

When holes are to be located on a circle, the diameter of the circle should be given so as to fix the exact center of each hole. The size and position of each hole are noted on the drawing, figure 14-3A. If more than one hole is the same diameter, then a notation may be used to indicate this fact, figure 14-3B.

For example, the notation ".500 REAM – 5 HOLES" means that the five holes on the drawings are reamed 1/2" in diameter.

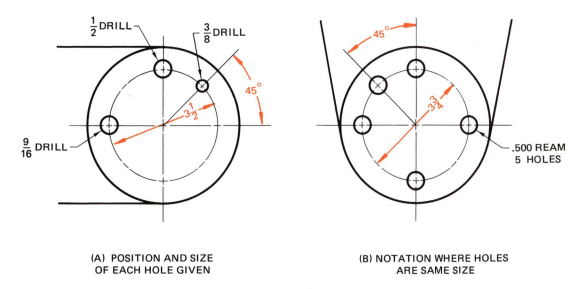

(A) POSITION AND SIZE
OF EACH HOLE GIVEN

(B) NOTATION WHERE HOLES
ARE SAME SIZE

FIGURE 14-3 TWO METHODS OF DIMENSIONING UNEQUALLY SPACED HOLES ON A CIRCLE

DIMENSIONING HOLES NOT ON A CIRCLE

Holes are often dimensioned in relation to one another or to a finished surface, rather than from a common center. Dimensions are usually given, in such cases, in the view which shows the shape of the holes, that is, square, round, or elongated. The preferred method of placing these dimensions is shown in figure 14-4A.

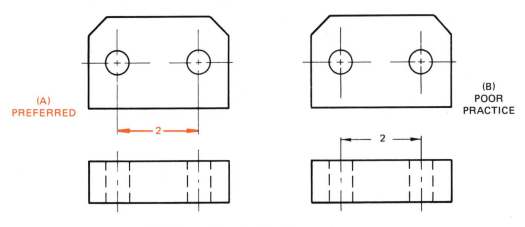

(A)
PREFERRED

(B)
POOR
PRACTICE

FIGURE 14-4 PLACING DIMENSIONS FOR HOLES

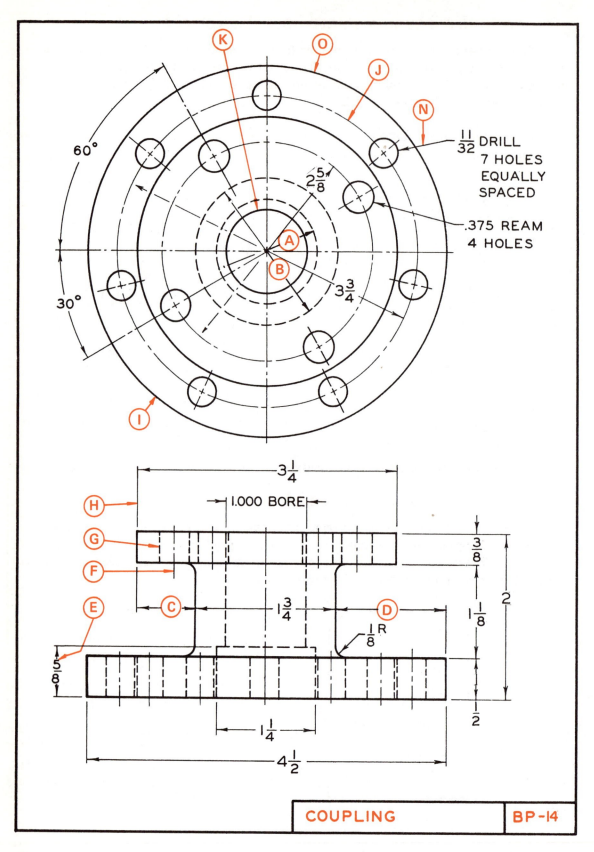

60°

30°

K   O   J   N

$\frac{11}{32}$ DRILL
7 HOLES
EQUALLY
SPACED

.375 REAM
4 HOLES

$2\frac{5}{8}$

A

B

$3\frac{3}{4}$

I

$3\frac{1}{4}$

1.000 BORE

H

G

F

$\frac{3}{8}$

E   C $1\frac{3}{4}$ D $1\frac{1}{8}$ 2

$\frac{1}{8}$ R

$\frac{5}{8}$

$\frac{1}{2}$

$1\frac{1}{4}$

$4\frac{1}{2}$

COUPLING   **BP-14**

COUPLING (BP-14)

1. Name the view which shows the width of the Coupling.

2. Name the view in which the holes are shown as circles.

3. Name the kind of line shown at (E) (F) (G) (H) (I) (J).

4. What circle represents the 4 1/2'' diameter flange?

5. What circle represents the 1'' bore diameter?

6. Name the kind of line shown at (N).

7. How many holes are to be drilled in the larger flange?

8. Indicate the drill size to be used.

9. Give the diameter circle on which the equally spaced holes are drilled in the larger flange.

10. How many holes are to be reamed in the smaller flange?

11. How deep is the 1 1/4'' DIA hole bored?

12. Give the diameter of the reamed holes.

13. State the angle with the horizontal center line used for locating the first clockwise reamed hole.

14. What is the overall thickness of the Coupling?

15. What is the diameter of the smaller flange?

16. What is the diameter of the circle (A) ? circle (B) ?

17. What is the length of the 1'' bored hole?

18. What is the thickness of the larger flange?

19. If a 5/16'' bolt is used in the drilled holes, what will be the clearance between the hole and the bolt?

20. Determine distances (C), (D).

ASSIGNMENT   UNIT 14

Student's Name _____

1. _____
2. _____
3. (E) _____
   (F) _____
   (G) _____
   (H) _____
   (I) _____
   (J) _____
4. _____
5. _____
6. _____
7. _____
8. _____
9. _____
10. _____
11. _____
12. _____
13. _____
14. _____
15. _____
16. (A) _____
    (B) _____
17. _____
18. _____
19. _____
20. (C) _____
    (D) _____

UNIT 15   DIMENSIONING LARGE ARCS AND BASE LINE DIMENSIONING

DIMENSIONING ARCS WITH CENTERS OUTSIDE THE DRAWING

When the center of an arc falls outside the limits of the drawing, a broken dimension line is used as illustrated in figure 15-1. This dimension line gives the size of the arc and indicates that the arc center lies on a center line outside the drawing. This technique is used, also, when a dimension line interferes with other parts of a drawing.

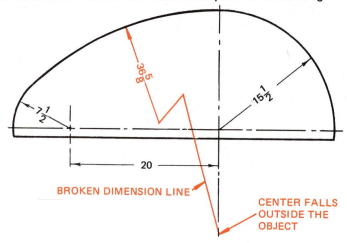

FIGURE 15-1 USING BROKEN DIMENSION LINE

BASE LINE DIMENSIONING

In base line dimensioning, all measurements are made from common finished surfaces called *base lines* or *reference lines*, figure 15-2. Base line dimensioning is used where accurate layout work to precision limits is required. Errors are not cumulative with this type of dimensioning because all measurements are taken from the base lines.

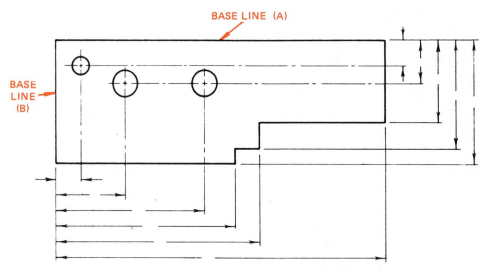

FIGURE 15-2 BASE LINE DIMENSIONING FROM TWO MACHINED EDGES

Dimensions and measurements may be taken from one or more base lines. In figure 15-2, the two base lines are at right angles to each other. The horizontal dimensions are measured from base line (B) which is a machined edge. The vertical dimensions are measured from surface (A) which is at right angles to surface (B) and is also a machined surface.

An application of base line dimensioning, where a center line is used as the reference line, is shown in figure 15-3A. Base line dimensioning may also be applied to irregular shapes such as the template shown in figure 15-3B.

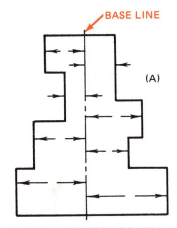

CENTER LINE USED AS BASE LINE

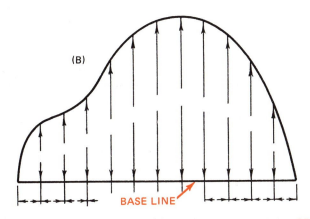

BASE LINE DIMENSIONING APPLIED TO IRREGULAR SHAPE

FIGURE 15-3 APPLICATIONS OF BASE LINE DIMENSIONING

Base line dimensions simplify the reading of a drawing and also permit greater accuracy in making the part.

SHOP DIMENSIONS

In most machine and metal shops, dimensions under 72 inches are usually stated in inches. By comparison, measurements for structural work and the building industry are usually given in feet and inches.

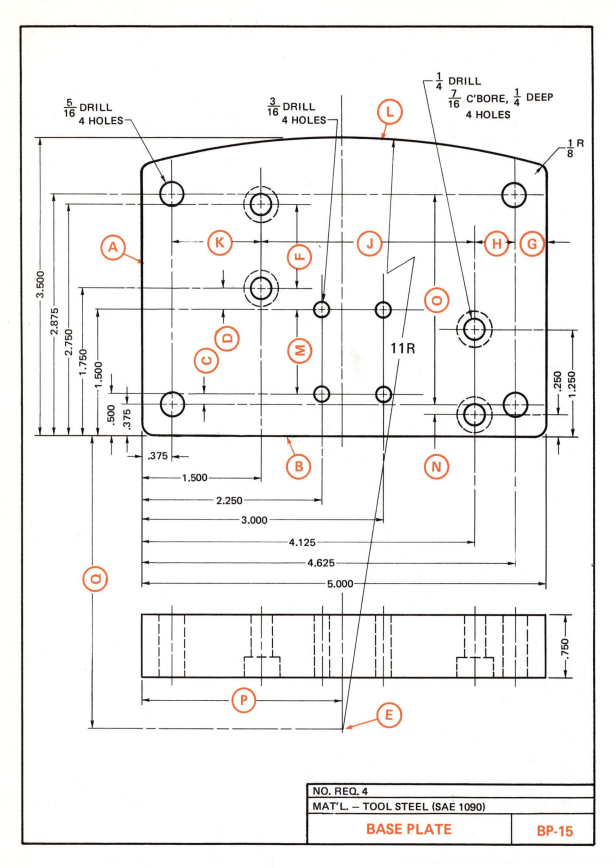

NO. REQ. 4

MAT'L. – TOOL STEEL (SAE 1090)

BASE PLATE | BP-15

BASE PLATE (BP-15)

1. Give the name of the part.

2. What material is used for the Base Plate?

3. How many parts are required?

4. What is the length of the Base Plate?

5. What is the width of the Base Plate?

6. What is the thickness of the Plate?

7. How many 5/16" holes are to be drilled?

8. How many 3/16" holes are to be drilled?

9. How many 1/4" holes are to be drilled?

10. Give (a) the diameter and (b) the depth of counterbore for the 1/4" holes.

11. What system of dimensioning is used on this drawing?

12. Give the letter of the base line in the Top View from which all vertical dimensions are taken.

13. Give the letter of the base line in the Top View from which all horizontal dimensions are taken.

14. Compute the following vertical dimensions: Ⓒ Ⓓ Ⓜ Ⓕ.

15. Compute the following horizontal dimensions: Ⓖ Ⓗ Ⓙ Ⓚ.

16. Compute dimensions Ⓝ and Ⓞ.

17. Give the radius to which the corners are rounded.

18. What is the radius of arc Ⓛ?

19. What letter indicates the center for arc Ⓛ?

20. Compute dimensions Ⓟ and Ⓠ.

ASSIGNMENT   UNIT 15

Student's Name _____

1. _____
2. _____
3. _____
4. _____
5. _____
6. _____
7. _____
8. _____
9. _____
10. (a)_____ (b)_____
11. _____
12. _____
13. _____
14. Ⓒ = _____
    Ⓓ = _____
    Ⓜ = _____
    Ⓕ = _____
15. Ⓖ = _____
    Ⓗ = _____
    Ⓙ = _____
    Ⓚ = _____
16. Ⓝ = _____
    Ⓞ = _____
17. _____
18. _____
19. _____
20. Ⓟ = _____
    Ⓠ = _____

TOLERANCES, FRACTIONAL AND ANGULAR DIMENSIONS

TOLERANCES

As a part is planned, the designer must consider (1) its function either as a separate unit or as a part which must move in a fixed position in relation to other parts, (2) the operations required to produce the part, (3) the material to be used, (4) the quantity to be produced, and (5) the cost. Each of these factors influences the degree of accuracy to which a part is machined.

The dimensions given on a drawing are an indication of what the limits of accuracy are. These limits are called *tolerances*. If a part does not require a high degree of accuracy, the drawing may specify the tolerances to which the part is to be held in terms of *fractional dimensions*. More precisely machined parts require that the accuracy be given in terms of *decimal tolerances*.

SPECIFYING FRACTIONAL TOLERANCES

The note in figure 16-1, LIMITS ON FRACTIONAL DIMENSIONS ARE ± 1/64″, indicates that the dimension given in fractions on the drawing may be machined any size between a 64th of an inch larger to a 64th of an inch smaller than the specified size.

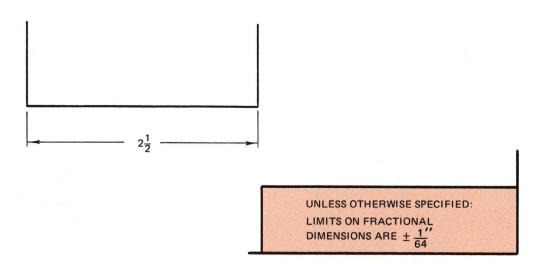

FIGURE 16-1 FRACTIONAL TOLERANCES APPLIED

For example, on the 2 1/2″ dimension in figure 16-1:

1. The tolerance given on the drawing is ± 1/64″.

2. The largest size to which the part may be machined is 2 1/2″ + 1/64″ = 2 33/64″

3. The smallest size to which the part may be machined is 2 1/2″ – 1/64″ = 2 31/64″

The larger size is called the *upper limit;* the smaller size is called the *lower limit.*

ANGULAR DIMENSIONS

Angles are dimensioned in degrees or parts of a degree.

1. Each degree is one three hundred sixtieth of a circle (1/360).

2. The degree may be divided into smaller units called *minutes.* There are 60 minutes in each degree.

3. Each minute may be divided into smaller units called *seconds.* There are 60 seconds in each minute.

To simplify the dimensioning of angles, symbols are used to indicate degrees, minutes and seconds, figure 16-2. For example, twelve degrees, sixteen minutes and five seconds can also be written 12° 16′ 5″.

	SYMBOL
DEGREES	°
MINUTES	′
SECONDS	″

FIGURE 16-2 SYMBOLS USED FOR DIMENSIONING ANGLES

SPECIFYING ANGULAR TOLERANCES

The tolerance on an angular dimension may be given in a note on the drawing as shown in figure 16-3. The tolerance may also be shown on the angular dimension itself, figure 16-4.

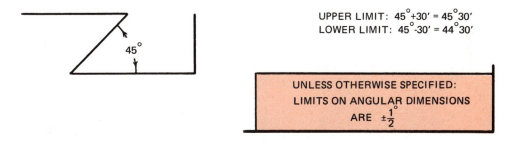

UPPER LIMIT: $45° + 30′ = 45°30′$
LOWER LIMIT: $45° - 30′ = 44°30′$

UNLESS OTHERWISE SPECIFIED:
LIMITS ON ANGULAR DIMENSIONS
ARE $\pm \frac{1°}{2}$

FIGURE 16-3 TOLERANCE SPECIFIED AS A NOTE

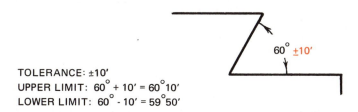

TOLERANCE: ±10′
UPPER LIMIT: $60° + 10′ = 60°10′$
LOWER LIMIT: $60° - 10′ = 59°50′$

FIGURE 16-4 TOLERANCE SPECIFIED ON ANGULAR DIMENSION

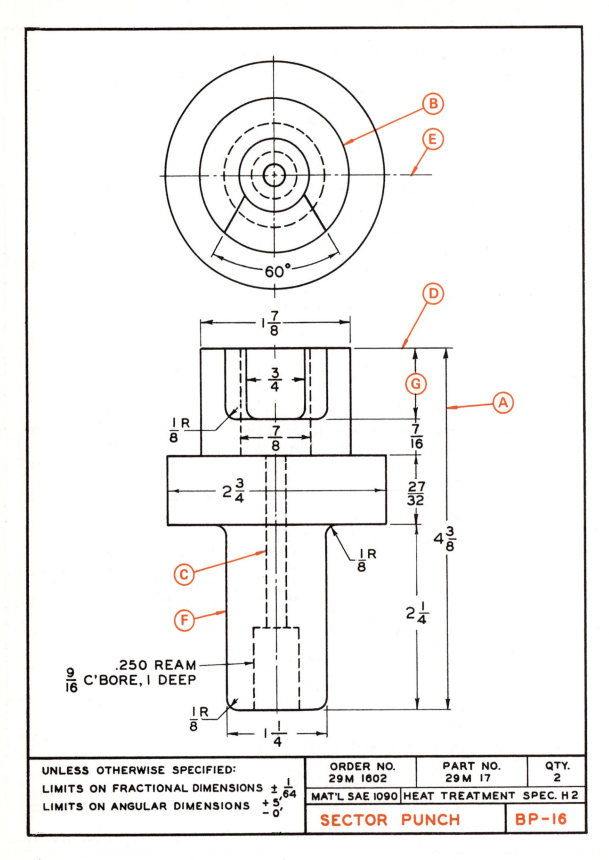

60°

1 7/8

3/4

1/8 R

7/8

2 3/4

1/8 R

C

F

.250 REAM
9/16 C'BORE, 1 DEEP

1/8 R

1 1/4

7/16

27/32

4 3/8

2 1/4

B

E

D

G

A

UNLESS OTHERWISE SPECIFIED:	ORDER NO. 29M 1602	PART NO. 29M 17	QTY. 2
LIMITS ON FRACTIONAL DIMENSIONS ± 1/64	MAT'L SAE 1090	HEAT TREATMENT SPEC. H2	
LIMITS ON ANGULAR DIMENSIONS + 5', − 0'	SECTOR PUNCH		BP-16

SECTOR PUNCH (BP-16)

1. What letter is used to denote a

   a. Hidden edge line

   b. Dimension line

   c. Extension line

   d. Center line

2. Determine dimension (G) .

3. What is the diameter of the reamed pilot hole for the counterbore?

4. Give the diameter and depth of the counterbore.

5. What are the upper and lower limits of tolerance for fractional dimensions?

6. What limit of tolerance is specified for angular dimensions?

7. What is the largest size to which the 2 3/4″ diameter can be turned?

8. What is the lower limit to which the 2 3/4″ diameter can be machined?

9. Give the upper limit to which diameter (B) may be machined.

10. Give the upper and lower limit on the diameter for shank (F) .

11. If shank (F) is turned to the upper limit length, how long will it be?

12. If shank (F) is machined 2 3/16″ long, how much under the lower limit size will it be?

13. How much over the upper limit will the shank be if it is 2 5/16″ long?

14. What is the upper limit of accuracy for the 60° angle?

15. If the height of the 1 7/8″ diameter punch measures 1 9/32″, is it over, under or within the specified limits of accuracy?

ASSIGNMENT   UNIT 16

Student's Name _____

1. (a) _____

   (b) _____

   (c) _____

   (d) _____

2. _____

3. _____

4. Diameter _____

   Depth _____

5. Upper _____

   Lower _____

6. _____

7. _____

8. _____

9. _____

10. Upper _____

    Lower _____

11. _____

12. _____

13. _____

14. _____

15. _____

UNILATERAL AND BILATERAL TOLERANCES, DECIMAL DIMENSIONS AND TOLERANCES

UNILATERAL AND BILATERAL TOLERANCES

The limits of accuracy to which a part is to be produced may fall within one of two classifications of tolerances. A dimension is said to have a *unilateral* (single) tolerance when the total tolerance is in one direction only, either (+) or (–). The examples of unilateral tolerances shown in figure 17-1 indicate that part (A) meets standards of accuracy when the basic dimension varies in one direction only and is between 3″ and 3 1/64″; part (B) may vary from 2 7/16″ to 2 27/64″; and angle (C) may vary between 60° and 59° 45′.

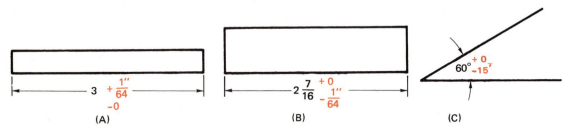

FIGURE 17-1 EXAMPLES OF UNILATERAL TOLERANCES

Bilateral tolerances applied to dimensions mean that the dimensions may vary from a larger size (+) to a smaller size (–) than the basic dimension. In other words, the basic dimension may vary in both directions. If equal tolerances such as $\pm$ 1/64″ are applied to the previous illustrations, then the basic 3″ dimension may vary between 3 1/64″ and 2 63/64″ for (A). The basic 2 7/16″ dimension in (B) is acceptable within a range of 2 29/64″ and 2 27/64″. The 60° angle in (C) may range between 60° 15′ and 59° 45′. These bilateral tolerances are shown in figure 17-2A, B and C.

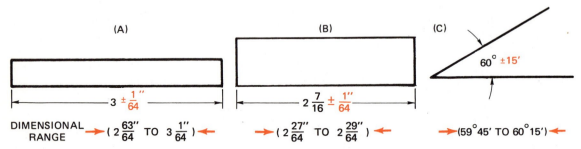

FIGURE 17-2 EXAMPLES OF BILATERAL TOLERANCES

When the dimensions within the tolerance limits appear on a drawing, they are expressed as a range from the smaller to the larger dimension as indicated in figure 17-2.

DECIMAL DIMENSIONS

The decimal system of dimensioning is widely used in industry because of the ease with which computations can be made. In addition, the dimension can be measured with precision instruments to a high degree of accuracy.

Dimensions in the decimal system can be read quickly and accurately in thousandths, 1/1000″ = (.001″), in ten thousandths, 1/10,000 = (.0001″), and in even finer divisions if necessary.

SPECIFYING DECIMAL TOLERANCES

Decimal tolerances can be applied in both the English and the metric systems of measurement. Tolerances on decimal dimensions may be given on a drawing in several ways. One of the common methods of specifying a tolerance that applies on all dimensions is to use a note, figure 17-3.

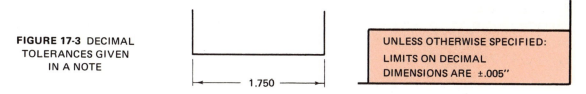

FIGURE 17-3 DECIMAL TOLERANCES GIVEN IN A NOTE

UNLESS OTHERWISE SPECIFIED:

LIMITS ON DECIMAL DIMENSIONS ARE ±.005"

For example, the 1.750" dimension in the figure may be machined to a size ranging from

$$1.750'' + .005'' = 1.755''$$
$$\text{TO}$$
$$1.750'' - .005'' = 1.745''$$

The larger size (1.755) is called the *upper limit.* The smaller size (1.745) is called the *lower limit.*

A tolerance on a decimal dimension also may be included as part of the dimension, as shown in figure 17-4.

FIGURE 17-4 DECIMAL TOLERANCE INCLUDED WITH DIMENSION

UPPER LIMIT   1.750" + .002" = 1.752"
LOWER LIMIT   1.750" - .002" = 1.748"

1.750 ±.002

Bilateral tolerances are not always equal in both directions. It is common practice for a drawing to include either a (+) tolerance or a (-) tolerance that is greater than the other.

In cases where the plus and minus tolerances are not the same, such as plus .001" and minus .002", the dimension may be shown on the drawing as in figure 17-5.

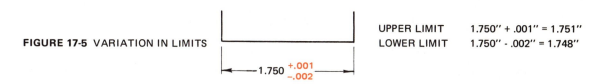

FIGURE 17-5 VARIATION IN LIMITS

UPPER LIMIT   1.750" + .001" = 1.751"
LOWER LIMIT   1.750" - .002" = 1.748"

1.750 +.001 / -.002

This same variation between the upper and lower limit can be given as in figure 17-6. The dimension above the line is the upper limit; the dimension below the line is the lower limit.

FIGURE 17-6 UPPER AND LOWER LIMIT DIMENSION

UPPER LIMIT   1.751"
LOWER LIMIT   1.748"

1.751
1.748

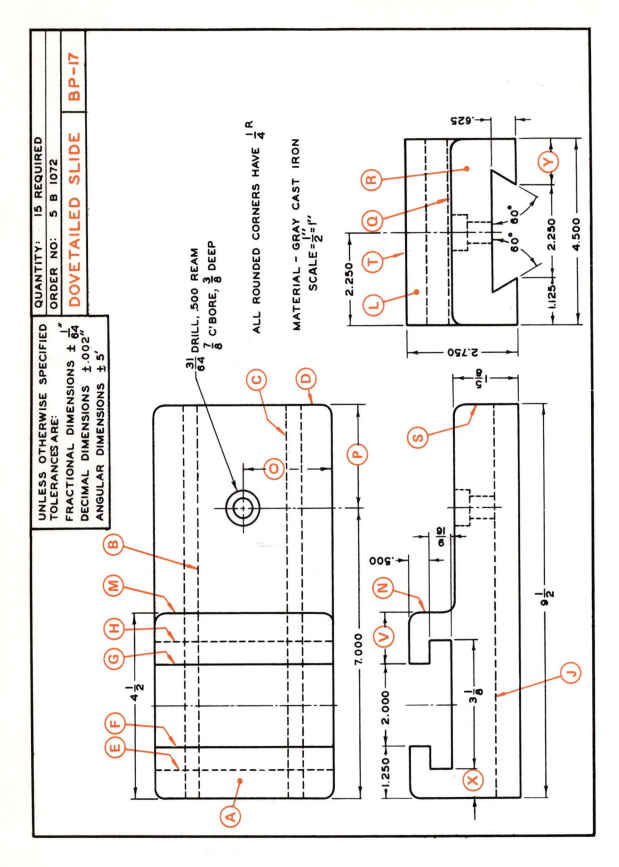

QUANTITY: 15 REQUIRED
ORDER NO: 5 B 1072

DOVETAILED SLIDE   BP-17

UNLESS OTHERWISE SPECIFIED
TOLERANCES ARE:
FRACTIONAL DIMENSIONS ± $\frac{1}{64}$"
DECIMAL DIMENSIONS ±.002"
ANGULAR DIMENSIONS ±5'

31 DRILL, .500 REAM
$\frac{7}{8}$ C'BORE, $\frac{3}{8}$ DEEP

ALL ROUNDED CORNERS HAVE $\frac{1}{4}$ R

MATERIAL – GRAY CAST IRON
SCALE= $\frac{1"}{2}$ =1"

DOVETAILED SLIDE (BP-17)

1. What type of lines are (B) , (C) , (H) , (E) and (J) ?

2. What tolerance is allowed on
   a. Fractional dimensions?
   b. Decimal dimensions?
   c. Angular dimensions?

3. What is the minimum overall height or thickness?

4. Give the upper limit dimension for the 60° angle.

5. Give the upper and lower limit dimensions for (P) .

6. What is the maximum depth to which the counterbored hole can be bored?

7. What line in the top view represents surface (R) of the side view?

8. What line in the front view represents surface (L) ?

9. What line in the side view represents surface (A) of the top view?

10. What dimension indicates how far line (J) is from the base of the slide?

11. What two lines in the top view indicate the opening of the dovetail?

12. How wide is the opening in the dovetail?

13. At what angle to the horizontal is the dovetail cut?

14. Give dimension (Y) .

15. To what depth into the piece is the dovetail cut?

16. What is the vertical distance from surface (Q) to surface (T) ?

17. What is the upper limit dimension between surfaces (F) and (G) ?

18. What is the full depth of the tee slot?

19. Compute dimensions (V) and (X) .

20. What is the horizontal distance from line (N) to line (S) ?

21. What classification of tolerances applies to all dimensions?

22. Change the fractional, decimal, and angular tolerances so that only the (–) tolerances apply. Then, determine the upper and lower limit dimensions for:
    a. The angular dimension
    b. The distance between surfaces (F) and (G) .
    c. Distance (P) .

ASSIGNMENT UNIT 17

Student's Name _____

1. _____	11. _____
2. a. _____	12. _____
b. _____	13. _____
c. _____	14. _____
3. _____	15. _____
4. _____	16. _____
5. _____	17. _____
_____	18. _____
6. _____	19. _____
7. _____	_____
8. _____	20. _____
9. _____	21. _____
10. _____	_____
22. a. _____	
b. _____	
c. _____	

UNIT 18 *REPRESENTING AND DIMENSIONING SCREW THREADS*

Screw threads are used widely (1) to fasten two or more parts securely in position, (2) to transmit power (such as a feed screw on a machine), and (3) to produce motion in an instrument in order to take precision measurements.

THE UNIFIED AND THE AMERICAN NATIONAL FORM THREAD

The shape or profile of the thread is referred to as the *thread form* One of the most common thread forms resembles a "V". Threads with an included angle of 60° originally were called "Sharp V". Later, these threads were called "U.S. Standard", "American National", and "Unified" threads. Changes and improvements in the thread forms have been made over the years through standards which have been established by professional organizations. These include the National Screw Thread Commission, the American Standards Association, the U.S. Standards Institute, and (currently) the American National Standards Institute (ANSI).

The most commonly used thread forms are the *Unified* and the *American National.* The symbol "UN" is found on drawings to designate the Unified form, and "N" designates the American National form. The only difference between these two forms is in the shape of the top (crest) and the bottom (root) of the thread. Both the crest and root of the American National thread form are flat. In contrast, the crest of the Unified thread form may be either flat or rounded, and the root is always rounded. The characteristics of the two thread forms are shown in figure 18-1.

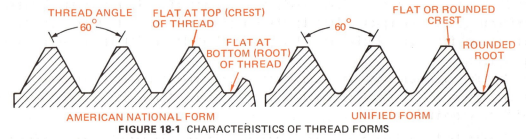

FIGURE 18-1 CHARACTERISTICS OF THREAD FORMS

COMMON THREAD FORMS

Four common thread forms that use the 60° included angle are represented pictorially in figure 18-2 as (A) the Sharp V, (B) Unified, (C) American National, and (D) Stub. The thread form is selected according to use. For instance, the 60° Stub thread is used where the depth of the Unified or American National form may be too deep for a particular part.

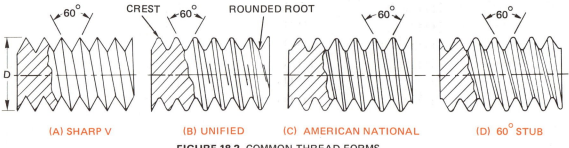

FIGURE 18-2 COMMON THREAD FORMS

A square form of thread, or a modified form, is used when great power or force is needed. The square form shown in figure 18-3A is called a *Square thread.* The more popular modified thread form has an included angle of 29° and is known as the *Acme thread,* figure 18-3B. The *Buttress thread,* (C), is used where power is to be transmitted in one direction. The *Knuckle thread,* (D), is usually found where a thread is molded (as in ceramic parts), or is rolled into thin metal parts (such as lamp sockets).

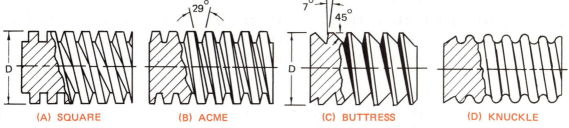

(A) SQUARE   (B) ACME   (C) BUTTRESS   (D) KNUCKLE

FIGURE 18-3 SQUARE AND MODIFIED THREAD FORMS

THREAD SERIES

Each thread form has a standard number of threads per inch for a given diameter. The term *thread series* designates the fineness or coarseness of the threads. For example, for both the Unified and the American National thread forms, there are six common series of screw threads. There is a *coarse* series (designated as "UNC" for Unified Coarse and "NC" for National Coarse); a *fine* series ("UNF" and "NF"); and an *extra fine* series ("UNEF" and NEF"). In addition, there are the *8 pitch, 12 pitch,* and *16 pitch* series. These series are identified on drawings as "8 UN" for the 8 pitch series in the Unified form, or "8 N" for the National form; as "12 UN" or "12 N", and as "16 UN" or "16 N", depending on the thread form.

Special conditions sometimes require that *nonstandard* or *special* thread series be used. In such cases, the drawings will include the designation "UNS" for Unified Special and "NS" for National Special.

Figure 18-4 is a summary of the six thread series and the designations for these series used on drawings.

	Designations on Drawings	
Thread Series	Unified System	American National System
Coarse	UNC	NC
Fine	UNF	NF
Extra Fine	UNEF	NEF
8 Pitch	8 UN	8 N
12 Pitch	12 UN	12 N
16 Pitch	16 UN	16 N

FIGURE 18-4 SUMMARY OF THREAD SERIES

REPRESENTING SCREW THREADS

Screw threads are further classified into two basic types: (1) *external threads* which are produced on the outside of a part, and (2) *internal threads* which are cut on the inside of the part. Letter symbols are sometimes used to designate the type: "A" for external threads and "B" for internal threads.

Internal and external threads may be represented on mechanical drawings by one of several methods: (1) a *pictorial* representation which shows the threads as they appear to the eye, (2) a *schematic* representation, or (3) a *simplified* representation. Figure 18-5 shows how each type of thread can be represented.

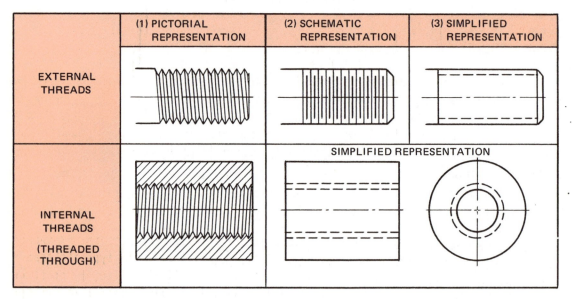

FIGURE 18-5 REPRESENTATION OF SCREW THREADS

DIMENSIONING SCREW THREADS

The representation of each thread is accompanied by a series of dimensions, letters, and numbers which, when combined, give full specifications for cutting and measuring the threads. The standard practices recommended by the American National Standards Institute (ANSI) for specifying and dimensioning external screw threads are shown in figure 18-6.

While the specifications as noted in figure 18-6 give all the information needed to describe a screw thread, the six items are not always used in the notation on a drawing. For example, the class of fit ⑤ may be covered by a general note which applies to all threaded parts. Such a note may appear elsewhere on the drawing. In other cases, the length of thread ⑥ sometimes appears as a dimension instead of appearing in the thread notation.

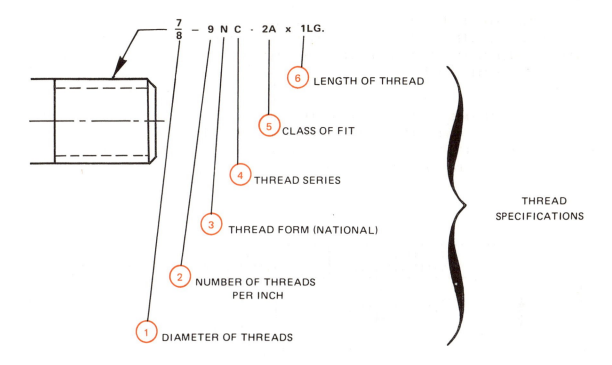

FIGURE 18-6 DIMENSIONING SCREW THREADS

PIPE THREAD REPRESENTATION

In addition to the screw threads just covered, there are two other common types of threads that are used on pipes. One type is the *Straight pipe thread.* This type of thread is noted on a drawing by the diameter of the thread followed by "NPS". Thus, the notation, 1" – NPS, indicates that (a) the part contains the standard number of threads in the pipe series for a 1" diameter, and (b) the threads are "straight".

In the second type of pipe thread, the threads are cut along a standard taper. The tapered pipe threads are used where a tight, leakproof seal is needed between the parts that are joined. Such threads are called *National Pipe Taper* threads, designated by "NPT". They are specified on pictorial, schematic, or simplified drawings by the diameter and the type. The notation, 1" – NPT, means (a) that there are the standard number of threads on the part for the 1" diameter in the pipe thread series, and (b) both the internal and external threads are cut on the standard pipe taper.

While a number of different forms and thread series have been described, only the commonly used Unified and National Coarse threads are included in this basic text.

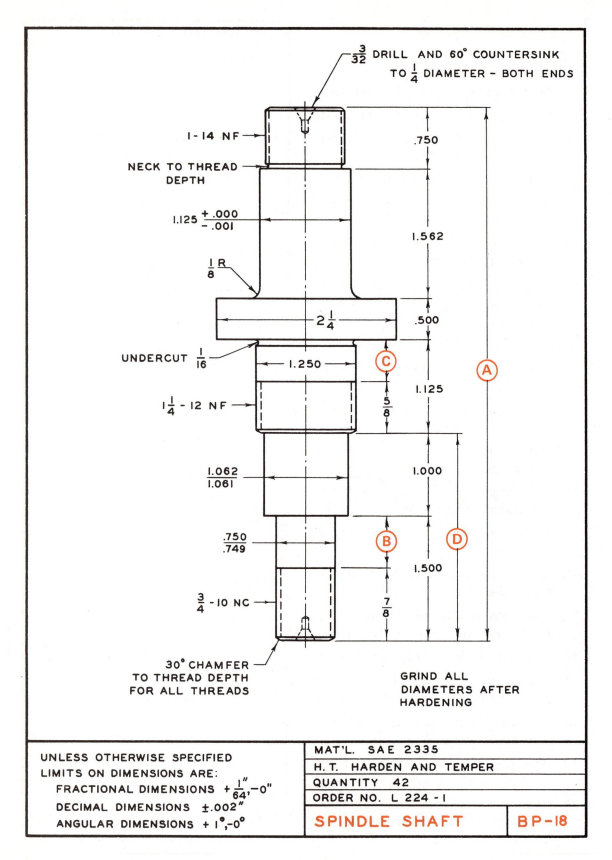

$\frac{3}{32}$ DRILL AND 60° COUNTERSINK
TO $\frac{1}{4}$ DIAMETER – BOTH ENDS

1-14 NF

NECK TO THREAD
DEPTH

1.125 $\begin{array}{c}+ .000\\- .001\end{array}$

.750

1.562

$\frac{1}{8}$ R

2 $\frac{1}{4}$

.500

UNDERCUT $\frac{1}{16}$

C

1.250

1 $\frac{1}{4}$ - 12 NF

1.125

$\frac{5}{8}$

A

$\frac{1.062}{1.061}$

1.000

$\frac{.750}{.749}$

B

D

$\frac{3}{4}$ -10 NC

1.500

$\frac{7}{8}$

30° CHAMFER
TO THREAD DEPTH
FOR ALL THREADS

GRIND ALL
DIAMETERS AFTER
HARDENING

UNLESS OTHERWISE SPECIFIED
LIMITS ON DIMENSIONS ARE:
   FRACTIONAL DIMENSIONS $+\frac{1}{64}", -0"$
   DECIMAL DIMENSIONS $\pm.002"$
   ANGULAR DIMENSIONS $+ 1°, -0°$

MAT'L.	SAE 2335
H. T.	HARDEN AND TEMPER
QUANTITY	42
ORDER NO.	L 224 - 1

SPINDLE SHAFT   BP-18

SPINDLE SHAFT (BP-18)

1. What material is used for the part?

2. Give the overall length of the shaft.

3. What system of representation is used for the threaded portions?

4. At how many places are threads cut?

5. Start at the bottom of the part and give all the thread diameters.

6. Name the two thread series that the letters NC and NF specify.

7. How many threads per inch are to be cut on the 3/4", 1 1/4" and 1" diameters?

8. Give dimensions (B), (C) and (D).

9. Give the upper and lower limit dimensions for the 3/4" threaded portion.

10. What is the length of the 3/4" threads? The 1 1/4" threads?

11. Give the upper and lower limit dimensions of the 1 1/16" diameter portion.

12. What angle are the chamfers at the starting end of each thread cut?

13. What tolerance is specified for angular dimensions?

14. What is the upper and lower limit of size on the 1 1/8" diameter?

15. How long is that part of the Shaft which has the 1 1/4" – 12 thread?

16. Give the angle of the countersink.

17. What is the largest diameter that the 2 1/4" diameter can be machined to?

18. Give the diameter to which the center holes are countersunk.

19. How deep is the undercut on the 1 1/4 diameter?

20. Name the final machining operation for all diameters after the part is heat treated.

21. Classify the tolerances for the fractional and angular dimensions.

ASSIGNMENT   UNIT 18

Student's Name _____

1. _____   9. Upper _____

2. _____   Lower _____

3. _____   10. 3/4" _____

   _____   1 1/4" _____

4. _____   11. Upper _____

5. _____   Lower _____

   _____   12. _____

   _____   13. _____

6. NC _____   14. Upper _____

   _____   Lower _____

   NF _____   15. _____

   _____   16. _____

7. 3/4" _____   17. _____

   1 1/4" _____   18. _____

   1" _____   19. _____

8. (B) _____   20. _____

   (C) _____   21. _____

   (D) _____   _____

REPRESENTING AND SPECIFYING INTERNAL AND LEFT-HAND THREADS

REPRESENTATION OF INTERNAL THREADS

One of the most practical and widely used methods of producing internal threads is to cut them with a round, formed thread-cutting tool called a *tap.* The tap is inserted in a hole which is the same diameter as the root diameter of the thread to be produced. As the tap with its multiple cutting edges is turned, it advances into the hole to cut a thread. The thread is a specified size and shape to correspond with a mating threaded part. This process is called *tapping* and the hole which is threaded is called a *tapped hole.* When the hole is a drilled hole, the drill is called a *tap drill.*

A part may be threaded internally either throughout its entire length or to a specified depth either by tapping or another machining process. Some threads are *bottomed* at the same depth as the tap drill. In other cases, the tap drill hole may be deeper. Both schematic and simplified forms of representing such threads are used in figure 19-1. Section (A) illustrates through threads; Section (B) shows internal threads that are bottomed, and Section (C) shows holes that are threaded to a depth less than the tap drill depth.

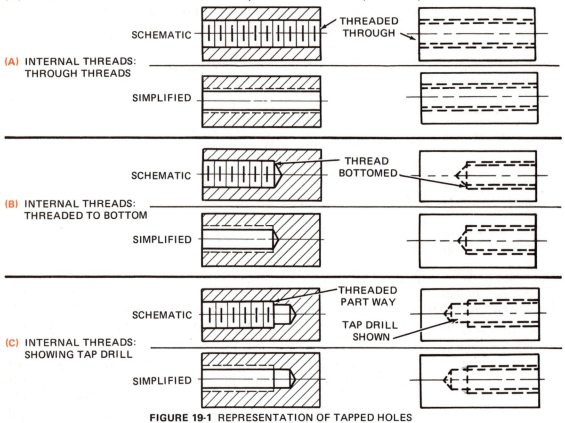

FIGURE 19-1 REPRESENTATION OF TAPPED HOLES

DIMENSIONING A THREADED HOLE

The same system of dimensioning that is used to specify external threads applies to internal threads. However, in the case of internal threads, the thread length is specified as the *depth of thread.* The recommended dimensioning of a tapped hole is illustrated in figure 19-2.

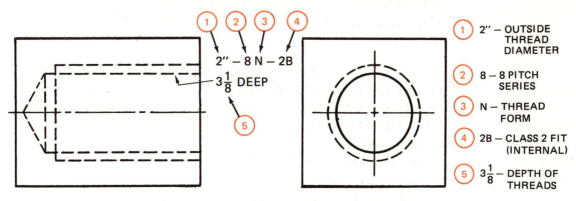

FIGURE 19-2 DIMENSIONING A TAPPED HOLE

CLASS OF FIT: UNIFIED AND AMERICAN NATIONAL FORM THREADS

There are three regular classes of fits for external and internal threads. The variation is from the loose *Class 1* fit to *Class 3* which requires a high degree of accuracy. Fits that are Class 1A (where "A" designates external threads) and Class 1B ("B" for internal threads) provide the greatest allowance and tolerances between the fitted parts. The Class 2A and Class 2B fit is the most widely used as it provides an acceptable minimum of clearance between the mating parts. The Class 3A and Class 3B fit is used for great accuracy. When the class of fit is given, it is usually included on the drawing as part of the screw thread notation, figure 19-3.

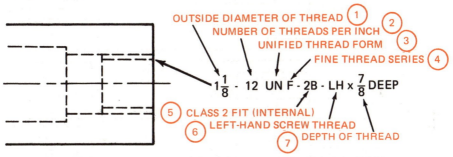

FIGURE 19-3 MEANING OF INTERNAL THREAD SPECIFICATIONS

SPECIFYING LEFT-HAND THREADS

Screw threads are cut either right-hand or left-hand depending on the application, figure 19-4. As the terms imply, a right-hand thread is advanced by turning clockwise, or to the right; the left-hand thread is advanced by turning counterclockwise, or to the left.

FIGURE 19-4 EXAMPLES OF RIGHT-AND LEFT-HAND THREADS

No notation is made on a drawing for right-hand threads as this direction of thread is assumed, unless otherwise noted. However, the letters LH are included on the drawing specifications to indicate when a left-hand thread is required as shown in figure 19-3 by the LH notation at ⑥.

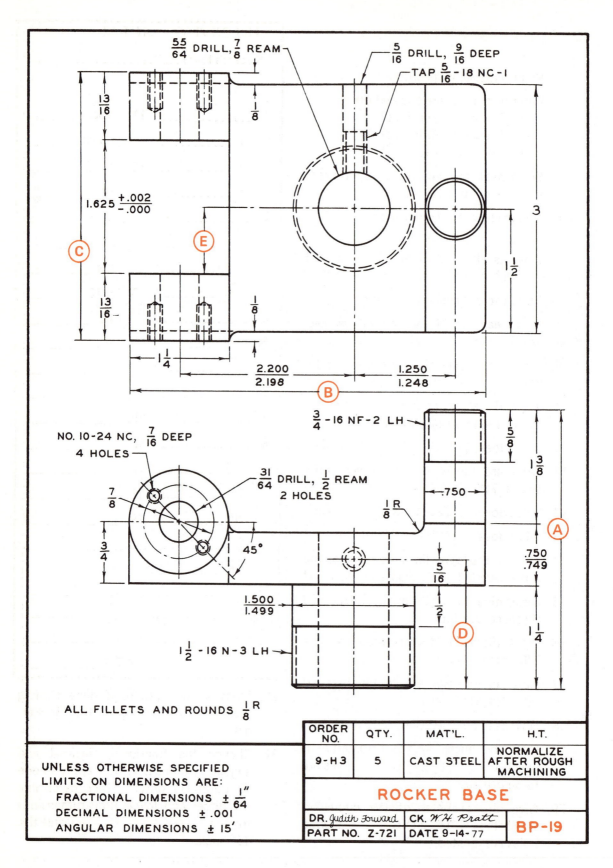

$\frac{55}{64}$ DRILL, $\frac{7}{8}$ REAM

$\frac{5}{16}$ DRILL, $\frac{9}{16}$ DEEP

TAP $\frac{5}{16}$ -18 NC-1

$\frac{13}{16}$

$\frac{13}{16}$

$1.625 \begin{smallmatrix}+.002\\-.000\end{smallmatrix}$

$\frac{1}{8}$

$\frac{1}{8}$

C

E

3

$1\frac{1}{2}$

$1\frac{1}{4}$

$\frac{2.200}{2.198}$

$\frac{1.250}{1.248}$

B

NO. 10-24 NC, $\frac{7}{16}$ DEEP
4 HOLES

$\frac{31}{64}$ DRILL, $\frac{1}{2}$ REAM
2 HOLES

$\frac{7}{8}$

$\frac{3}{4}$

45°

$\frac{1}{8}$ R

$\frac{3}{4}$ -16 NF-2 LH

$\frac{5}{8}$

$1\frac{3}{8}$

.750

A

$\frac{.750}{.749}$

$\frac{1.500}{1.499}$

$\frac{5}{16}$

$\frac{1}{2}$

D

$1\frac{1}{4}$

$1\frac{1}{2}$ -16 N-3 LH

ALL FILLETS AND ROUNDS $\frac{1}{8}$ R

ORDER NO.	QTY.	MAT'L.	H.T.
9-H3	5	CAST STEEL	NORMALIZE AFTER ROUGH MACHINING

UNLESS OTHERWISE SPECIFIED
LIMITS ON DIMENSIONS ARE:
  FRACTIONAL DIMENSIONS $\pm \frac{1}{64}"$
  DECIMAL DIMENSIONS $\pm$ .001
  ANGULAR DIMENSIONS $\pm$ 15′

ROCKER BASE

DR. Judith Forward	CK. W.H. Pratt	BP-19
PART NO. Z-721	DATE 9-14-77	

ROCKER BASE (BP-19)

1. What material is specified?

2. What tolerances are allowed on:
   - a. Decimal dimensions?
   - b. Fractional dimensions?
   - c. Angular dimensions?

3. What heat-treating process is required after rough machining?

4. Determine overall dimensions (A) (B) (C) .

5. What is the radius of all fillets and rounds?

6. Compute dimensions (D) and (E) .

7. How many holes are to be reamed 1/2"?

8. How many external threads are to be cut?

9. What thread series is used for the internal and external threads?

10. What does 3/4 – 16NF – 2LH mean?

11. What are the upper and lower limits of the .750 diameter portion?

12. What does 1 1/2 – 16N – 2LH mean?

13. What does 5/16 – 18NC – 1 mean?

14. What is the lower limit diameter of the unthreaded 1 1/2" diameter portion?

15. Determine the length of the 1 1/2" –16 threaded portion.

16. What diameter drill is used for the 7/8" reamed hole?

17. How many holes are to be threaded 10 – 24NC?

18. How deep are the holes to be threaded?

19. Give the angle to the horizontal at which the 10 – 24NC holes are to be drilled.

20. Give the diameter of the circle on which the 10 – 24NC tapped holes are located.

ASSIGNMENT   UNIT 19

Student's Name _____

1. _____   11. Upper _____
2. a. _____   Lower _____
   b. _____   12. 1 1/2 _____
   c. _____   16 _____
3. _____   N _____
4. (A) _____   2 _____
   (B) _____   LH _____
   (C) _____   13. 5/16 _____
5. _____   18 _____
6. (D) _____   NC _____
   (E) _____   1 _____
7. _____   14. _____
8. _____   15. _____
9. _____   16. _____
10. 3/4 _____   17. _____
    16 _____   18. _____
    NF _____   19. _____
    2 _____   20. _____
    LH _____
21. _____
22. (A) _____   (D) _____
    (B) _____   (E) _____
    (C) _____   45° ⊿ _____

21. Identify the system of dimensioning used on the drawing of the Rocker base.

22. Change the fractional, decimal and angular tolerances so they apply in one direction (+) only. Then, determine the upper and lower limit dimensions for (A) (B) (C) (D) (E) and the 45° angle.

UNIT 20 DIMENSIONING TAPERS AND MACHINED SURFACES

Blueprints of parts that uniformly change in size along their length show that the part is *tapered.* On a round piece of work, the taper is the difference between the diameter at one point and a diameter farther along the length. The taper is usually specified by a note on the drawing which gives the TAPER PER FOOT or the TAPER PER INCH. For example, a taper of one-half inch per foot is expressed:

$$\frac{1}{2} \text{ TAPER PER FOOT}$$

The drawing may give the large and small diameters at the beginning and end of the taper or one diameter and the length of the taper, figure 20-1.

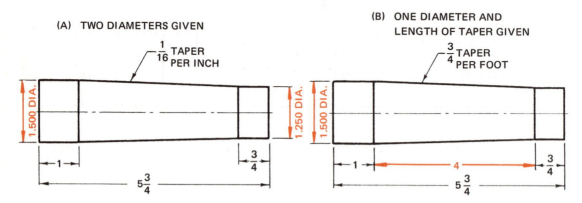

FIGURE 20-1 NOTES USED IN DIMENSIONING TAPERS

FINISHED SURFACES

Surfaces that are machined to a smooth finish and to accurate dimensions are called *finished surfaces.* A finish-mark symbol such as a 60° "V" on a drawing means that machining operations are to be performed on the indicated surfaces of castings, forgings, and welded parts.

The bottom of the "V" finish mark touches the surface to be machined. Figure 20-2 shows a steel forging. This same forging as it looks when machined is illustrated in figure 20-3. The working drawing, figure 20-4, shows how the finish marks are placed. Note that these marks appear on the hidden edge lines as well as on the object lines, with the exception of the small drilled holes. On large holes that require accurate machining, the "V" is used once again.

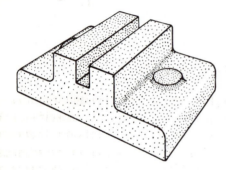

FIGURE 20-2 ROUGH FORGING

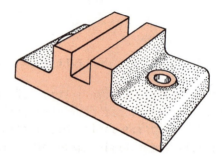

FIGURE 20-3 MACHINED FORGING

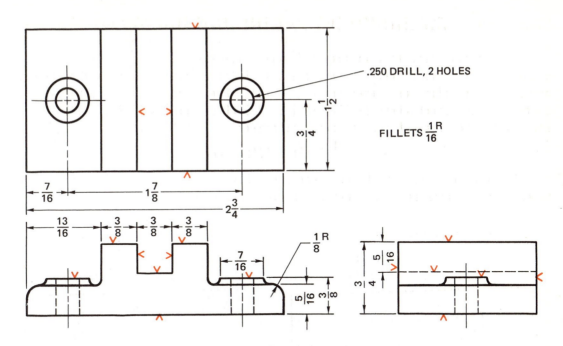

FIGURE 20-4 WORKING DRAWING OF FORGING SHOWING APPLICATION OF FINISH MARKS

FINISH ALL OVER

When a casting, forging, or welded part is to be finished all over, the drawing is simplified by omitting the finish marks and by adding the note: FINISH ALL OVER. The abbreviation FAO may be used in place of the phrase, finish all over.

SURFACE FINISH

Letters, numbers, and other symbols are used to indicate the machining operation to be performed on a surface. The degree of accuracy to which the machining must be held can also be indicated. In many industries, these symbols will appear in the opening of the "V". A few typical finish symbols are given in figure 20-5.

GRIND   MACHINE SMOOTH   ROUGH MACHINE   OLD SYMBOL DENOTING MACHINED SURFACE

FIGURE 20-5 EXAMPLES OF SURFACE FINISH SYMBOLS

A more accurate system of denoting the higher degree of accuracy required in machining parts has been developed. These more precise standards for specifying the quality of precision finished surfaces, established by the American National Standards Institute, are generally accepted throughout industry. They will be covered in the advanced blueprint reading text as more complex drawings and finer precision measurements are interpreted.

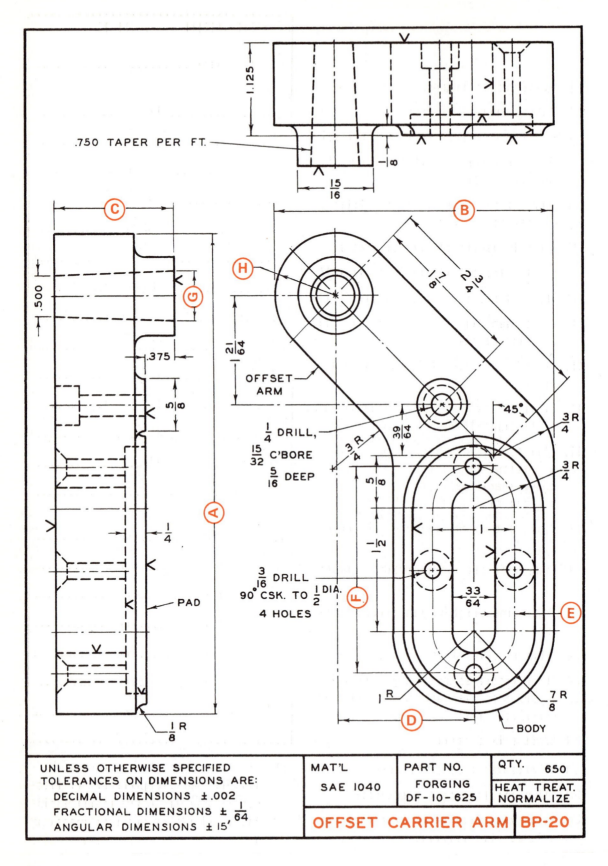

.750 TAPER PER FT.

1.125

15/16

1/8

C

.500

.375

G

5/8

1/4

A

PAD

1/8 R

B

H

OFFSET ARM

2 3/4

1 7/8

45°

21/64

1/4 DRILL,
15/32 C'BORE
5/16 DEEP

3 R 4

39/64

3/4 R

3/4 R

5/8

1

3/16 DRILL
90° CSK. TO 1/2 DIA.
4 HOLES

1 1/2

33/64

F.

E

1 R

7/8 R

D

BODY

UNLESS OTHERWISE SPECIFIED TOLERANCES ON DIMENSIONS ARE: DECIMAL DIMENSIONS ±.002 FRACTIONAL DIMENSIONS ± 1/64 ANGULAR DIMENSIONS ± 15'	MAT'L SAE 1040	PART NO. FORGING DF-10-625	QTY. 650
			HEAT TREAT. NORMALIZE
	OFFSET CARRIER ARM		BP-20

OFFSET CARRIER ARM (BP-20)

1. Name the three views.

2. What is the part number?

3. How many surfaces are to be machined?

4. Give the angle at which the arm is offset from the body.

5. What is the center-to-center distance of the offset arm?

6. Find the length of the elongated slot.

7. What is the overall length of the pad?

8. How is the counterbored hole specified?

9. What diameter drill is used for the countersunk holes?

10. What is the angle of the countersunk holes?

11. Compute the diameter at the large end of the tapered hole (G) .

12. What tolerance is allowed on:
    a. Decimal dimensions?
    b. Angular dimensions?
    c. Fractional dimensions?

13. What is the maximum overall height (A) ?

14. Determine the minimum overall width (B) .

15. Determine the maximum overall thickness (C) .

16. What are dimensions (D) and (H) ?

17. If the elongated slot is machined 1/2″, would it be over, under, or within the specified limits?

18. What is the distance (E) ?

19. Give center-to-center distance (F) .

20. What heat treatment is required?

21. What classification of tolerances applies to all dimensions?

ASSIGNMENT   UNIT 20

Student's Name _____

1. _____   12. (a) _____
   _____   (b) _____
   _____   (c) _____

2. _____   13. (A) = _____

3. _____   14. (B) = _____

4. _____   15. (C) = _____

5. _____   16. (D) = _____

6. _____   (H) = _____

7. _____   17. _____

8. _____   18. (E) = _____
   _____   19. (F) = _____

9. _____   20. _____

10. _____   21. _____

11. (G) = _____   _____

22. (A) = Min. _____ Max. _____

   (B) = Min. _____ Max. _____

   (C) = Min. _____ Max. _____

   (D) = Min. _____ Max. _____

   (E) = Min. _____ Max. _____

   (F) = Min. _____ Max. _____

   (H) = Min. _____ Max. _____

22. Use the appropriate fractional or decimal tolerance so it applies in one direction (+) only. Then, determine the minimum and maximum limit dimensions for (A)(B)(C)(D)(E)(F) and (H) .

DIMENSIONING WITH SHOP NOTES

The draftsperson often resorts to the use of notes on a drawing to convey to the mechanic all the information needed to make a part. Notes such as those used for drilling, reaming, counterboring, or countersinking holes are added to ordinary dimensions.

A note may consist of a very brief statement at the end of a leader, or it may be a complete sentence which gives an adequate picture of machining processes and all necessary dimensions. A note is found on a drawing near the part to which it refers. This unit includes the types of machining notes that are found on drawings of knurled surfaces, chamfers, grooves, and keyways. A sample of a typical change note is also given.

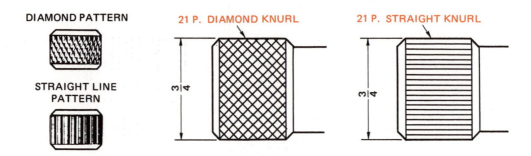

FIGURE 21-1 DIMENSIONS AND NOTES FOR KNURLED SURFACES

DIMENSIONING KNURLED SURFACES

The term *knurl* refers to a raised diamond-shaped surface or straight line impression in the surface of a part, figure 21-1. The dimensions and notes which furnish sufficient information for the technician to produce the knurled part are also shown in the figure. The pitch of the knurl, which gives the number of teeth per linear inch, is the size. The standard pitches are: coarse (14P), medium (21P), and fine (33P).

DIMENSIONING CHAMFERS AND GROOVES

When a surface must be cut away at a slight bevel, or have a groove cut into it, the drawing or blueprint gives complete machining information in the form illustrated in figures 21-2 and 21-3.

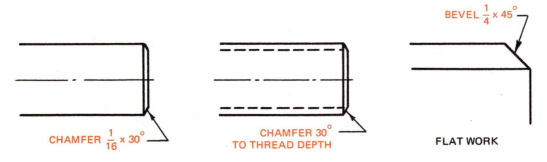

FIGURE 21-2 DIMENSIONING CHAMFERS AND BEVELS

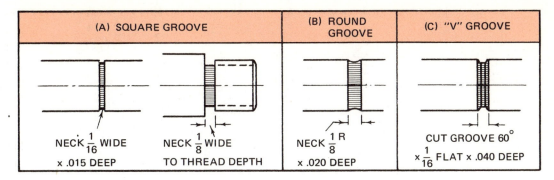

FIGURE 21-3 DIMENSIONING THREE COMMON TYPES OF GROOVES

KEYWAYS

A keyway refers to a groove cut into a shaft and a mating part, figure 21-4. A key is placed in this keyway to keep both parts in a fixed position and to prevent either part from turning.

Keyways for square and flat keys are dimensioned with the width of the keyway given first, followed by the depth. The method of dimensioning for square and flat keys is shown in figure 21-4.

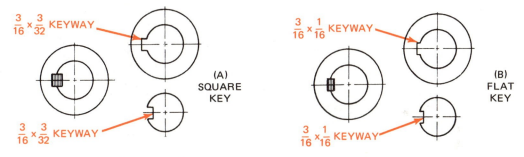

FIGURE 21-4 DIMENSIONING SQUARE AND FLAT KEYWAYS

CHANGE NOTES

The specifications and dimensions of parts are frequently changed on working drawings. An accurate record is usually made on the tracing and blueprint to indicate the nature of the change, the date, and who made the changes.

Changes that are minor in nature may be made without altering the original lines on the drawing. One of the easiest ways of making such changes is shown in figure 21-5.

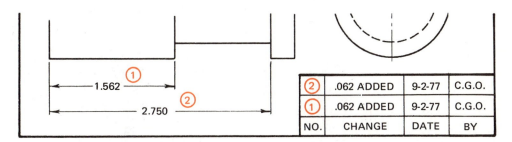

FIGURE 21-5 APPLICATION OF CHANGE NOTES

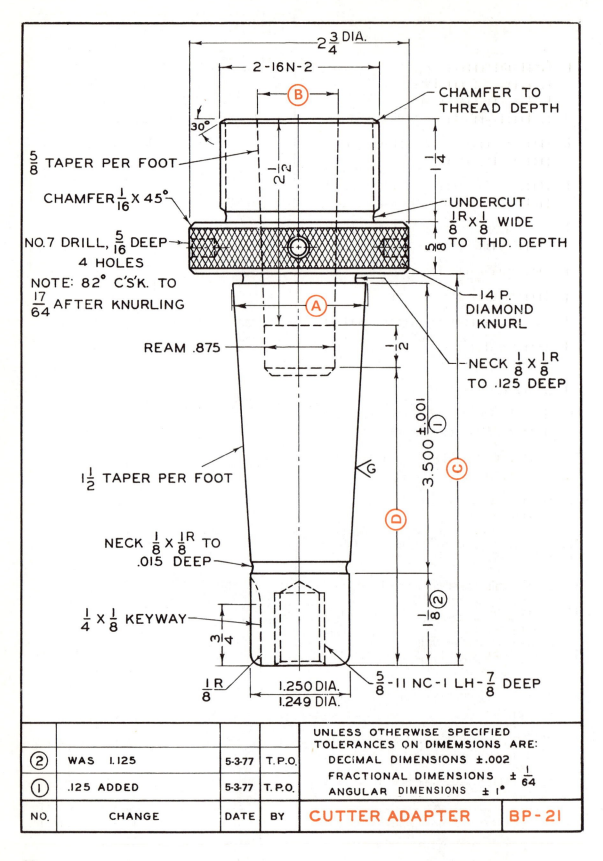

$2\frac{3}{4}$ DIA.

2-16N-2

Ⓑ

30°

$\frac{5}{8}$ TAPER PER FOOT

CHAMFER $\frac{1}{16}$ X 45°

NO.7 DRILL, $\frac{5}{16}$ DEEP
4 HOLES

NOTE: 82° C'S'K. TO
$\frac{17}{64}$ AFTER KNURLING

REAM .875

$1\frac{1}{2}$ TAPER PER FOOT

NECK $\frac{1}{8}$ X $\frac{1}{8}$R TO
.015 DEEP

$\frac{1}{4}$ X $\frac{1}{8}$ KEYWAY

$\frac{3}{4}$

$\frac{1}{8}$ R

1.250 DIA.
1.249 DIA.

$2\frac{1}{2}$

CHAMFER TO
THREAD DEPTH

$\frac{1}{4}$

UNDERCUT
$\frac{1}{8}$R X $\frac{1}{8}$ WIDE
TO THD. DEPTH

$\frac{5}{8}$

14 P.
DIAMOND
KNURL

NECK $\frac{1}{8}$ X $\frac{1}{8}$R
TO .125 DEEP

Ⓐ

$\frac{1}{2}$

3.500 ±.001 ①

Ⓒ

Ⓓ

G

$1\frac{1}{8}$ ②

$\frac{5}{8}$-11 NC-1 LH-$\frac{7}{8}$ DEEP

NO.	CHANGE	DATE	BY	UNLESS OTHERWISE SPECIFIED TOLERANCES ON DIMEMSIONS ARE: DECIMAL DIMENSIONS ±.002 FRACTIONAL DIMENSIONS ± $\frac{1}{64}$ ANGULAR DIMENSIONS ± 1°	
②	WAS 1.125	5-3-77	T.P.O.		
①	.125 ADDED	5-3-77	T.P.O.		
NO.	CHANGE	DATE	BY	**CUTTER ADAPTER**	**BP-21**

CUTTER ADAPTER (BP-21)

1. What tolerances are given for:
   a. Angular dimensions?
   b. Decimal dimensions?
   c. Fractional dimensions?

2. Give the exact specifications for the taper on the body.

3. What is the taper per inch for the body?

4. What is the diameter at the small end of the outside taper?

5. Determine dimension (A).

6. Give the taper for the hole.

7. What is the taper per inch for the hole?

8. Give the diameter at the small end of the inside taper.

9. Compute dimension (B).

10. Give the specifications for the outside threads on the nose portion.

11. What does the LH in the thread note for the shank end specify?

12. What is the class of fit for the 2″ threaded nose?

13. What operation is performed on the 2 3/4″ diameter?

14. How is this operation specified?

15. Determine the maximum diameter for the reamed hole.

16. Give the note for drilling the four holes in the largest diameter.

17. Specify the chamfer for the knurled portion.

18. Specify the angle of chamfer for the 2″ threaded nose.

19. How deep is the chamfer for the 2″ threads?

20. Give the original length of the tapered body before any change was made.

21. Compute maximum length of dimension (C).

22. What machining operation is indicated by the finish symbol G?

23. Determine dimension (D).

24. Give the dimensions of the keyway.

25. Determine the overall length of the adapter.

26. Change the decimal tolerance to apply unidirectionally as (+.003″). Then, compute the minimum and maximum dimensions for (A) and (B).

Student's Name _____

1. Angular ____ Decimal ____ Fractional ____
2. ____   15. ____
3. ____   16. ____
4. ____   ____
5. ____   17. ____
6. ____   18. ____
7. ____   19. Deep ____
8. ____   Angle ____
9. ____   20. ____
10. ____   21. ____
11. ____   22. ____
12. ____   23. ____
13. ____   24. Width ____
14. ____   Depth ____
       25. ____
26. (A) ____
    (B) ____

DATUMS, ORDINATE AND TABULAR DIMENSIONING

DATUMS

A *datum* is a reference feature from which dimensions are located and essential information is derived. A datum may be a point, line, plane, cylinder, or other exact feature. Datums are used in design, manufacturing, numerical control, and many other processes. Datums give location dimensions, furnish data for computations, and provide a reference source.

When a datum is specified, such as the two that are illustrated in figure 22-1, all features must be stated in relation to the datum reference. Different features of the part are located from the datum, not from other features. Datums must be clearly identified or easily recognizable. At least two, and often three, datums must be used to define or measure a part. Since all measurements are taken from datums (similar to those earlier used in base line dimensioning), errors in dimensioning are not cumulative.

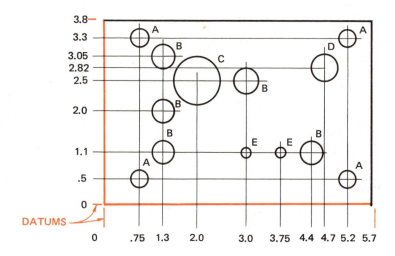

HOLE SIZE SYMBOL	A	B	C	D	E
HOLE DIAMETER	3/16	1/4	1	5/16	7/64

FIGURE 22-1 ORDINATE DIMENSIONING

ORDINATE DIMENSIONING AND NUMERICAL CONTROL MACHINE DRAWINGS

Ordinate dimensioning is a type of rectangular datum dimensioning. In ordinate dimensioning the dimensions are measured from two or three mutually related datum planes, figure 22-1. The datum planes are indicated as *zero coordinates*. Dimensions from the zero coordinates are represented on drawings as extension lines, without the use of dimension lines or arrowheads.

Specific features are located by the intersection of datum dimensions. Ordinate dimensioning is used when there would otherwise be a large number of dimensions and features and close tolerances are required. Datums and ordinate dimensioning are the foundation of numerically-controlled machine drawings and precision parts.

TABULAR DIMENSIONING

Tabular dimensioning is another form of rectangular datum dimensioning. As the term implies, dimensions from intersecting datum planes are given in a table, figure 22-2. Tabular dimensioning helps to eliminate possible errors which could result from incorrectly reading dimensions when a large number are included on a drawing.

Values of X and Y are measured along the respective datum lines from their intersection. The intersection is the origin of the coordinate. Tabular dimensioning is recommended where there are a great many repetitive features. These would make a dimensioned drawing difficult to read.

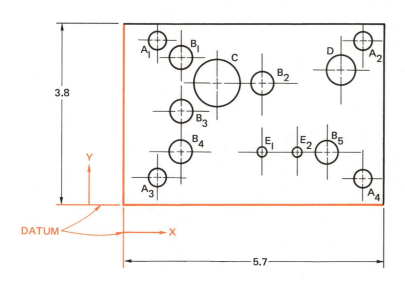

Hole Identification	Hole Size	Location X→	Y↑
A₁	3/16	.75	3.3
A₂	3/16	5.2	3.3
A₃	3/16	.75	.5
A₄	3/16	5.2	.5
B₁	1/4	1.3	3.05
B₂	1/4	3.0	2.5
B₃	1/4	1.3	2.0
B₄	1/4	1.3	1.1
B₅	1/4	4.4	1.1
C	1	2.0	2.5
D	5/16	4.7	2.82
E₁	7/64	3.0	1.1
E₂	7/64	3.75	1.1

FIGURE 22-2 COORDINATE CHART AND TABULAR DIMENSION DRAWING

COORDINATE CHARTS

The dimensions of a coordinate and features that are to be fabricated on coordinates are given in a coordinate chart, figure 22-2. Only those dimensions that originate at the datums are found in such a chart. The coordinates may specify sufficient information to fabricate the entire feature or only a portion of it.

Parts or components may be represented on drawings by ordinate or tabular dimensioning in the English or Metric system of measurement or in both systems.

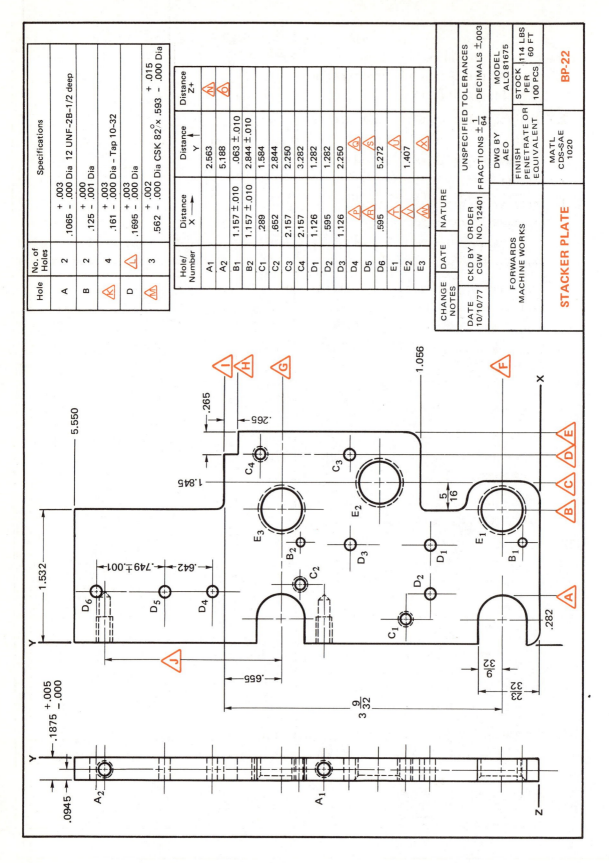

Hole	No. of Holes	Specifications
A	2	.1065 $+$ .003 $-$ .000 Dia 12 UNF-2B-1/2 deep
B	2	.125 $+$ .000 $-$ .001 Dia
	4	.161 $+$ .003 $-$ .000 Dia – Tap 10-32
D		.1695 $+$ .003 $-$ .000 Dia
	3	.562 $+$ .002 $-$ .000 Dia CSK 82°/x .593 $+$ .015 $-$ .000 Dia

Hole/ Number	Distance X	Distance Y	Distance Z+
A1		2.563	
A2		5.188	
B1	1.157 ± .010	.063 ± .010	
B2	1.157 ± .010	2.844 ± .010	
C1	.289	1.584	
C2	.652	2.844	
C3	2.157	2.250	
C4	2.157	3.282	
D1	1.126	1.282	
D2	.595	1.282	
D3	1.126	2.250	
D4			
D5		5.272	
D6	.595		
E1			
E2		1.407	
E3			

CHANGE NOTES	DATE	NATURE
DATE 10/10/77	CKD BY CGW	ORDER NO. 12401

UNSPECIFIED TOLERANCES
FRACTIONS $\pm \frac{1}{64}$ DECIMALS ±.003

DWG BY AEO

MODEL ALQ81675

FINISH PENETRATE OR EQUIVALENT

STOCK PER 100 PCS   114 LBS 60 FT

BP-22

FORWARDS MACHINE WORKS

MATL CDS-SAE 1020

STACKER PLATE

STACKER PLATE (BP-22)

1. Give the specification of the material in the Stacker Plates.

2. Determine the weight of 50 Stacker Plates.

3. Give the length of stock needed for 50 Stacker Plates.

4. State what modified systems of dimensioning are used.

5. Compute the maximum overall height and give the maximum thickness.

6. Determine the correct letter, designation or number for $\triangle K$, $\triangle L$, and $\triangle M$ in the specification chart.

7. Give the specifications for the .1065 Dia holes.

8. State why the $\triangle Z$ axis view is necessary.

9. Compute dimensions $\triangle N$ and $\triangle O$.

10. Determine the maximum Y axis distance between C_1 and C_4.

11. State what the hidden lines around hole (circle) E_3 represents.

12. Compute dimensions $\triangle A$, $\triangle B$, $\triangle C$, $\triangle D$, and $\triangle E$.

13. Determine dimensions $\triangle F$, $\triangle G$, $\triangle H$, $\triangle I$, and $\triangle J$.

14. Determine ordinate distances $\triangle P$, $\triangle Q$, $\triangle R$, and $\triangle S$.

15. Compute tabular dimensions $\triangle T$, $\triangle U$, $\triangle V$, $\triangle W$, and $\triangle X$.

16. Compute the minimum vertical distance between $\triangle I$ and D_4.

ASSIGNMENT   UNIT 22

Student's Name _____

1. _____

2. _____

3. _____

4. _____

5. Maximum   Maximum
   Height = _____   Thickness = _____

6. $\triangle K$ = ____ $\triangle L$ = ____ $\triangle M$ = ____

7. _____

8. _____

9. $\triangle N$ = _____ $\triangle O$ = _____

10. _____

11. _____

12. $\triangle A$ = _____ $\triangle B$ = _____
    $\triangle C$ = _____ $\triangle D$ = _____
    $\triangle E$ = _____

13. $\triangle F$ = _____ $\triangle G$ = _____
    $\triangle H$ = _____ $\triangle I$ = _____
    $\triangle J$ = _____

14. $\triangle P$ = _____ $\triangle Q$ = _____
    $\triangle R$ = _____ $\triangle S$ = _____

15. $\triangle T$ = _____ $\triangle U$ = _____
    $\triangle V$ = _____ $\triangle W$ = _____
    $\triangle X$ = _____

16. _____

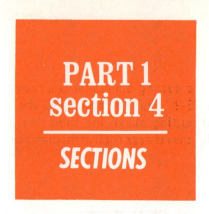

PART 1
section 4
SECTIONS

UNIT **23**

CUTTING PLANES, SECTION LINING AND FULL SECTIONS

An exterior view shows the object as it looks when seen from the outside. The inside details of such an object are shown on the drawing by hidden lines.

As the details inside the part become more complex, additional invisible lines are needed to show the hidden details accurately. This tends to make the drawing increasingly more difficult to interpret. One technique the draftsperson uses on such drawings to simplify them is to cut away a portion of the object. This exposes the inside surfaces. On cut-away sections, all of the edges that are visible are represented by visible edge of object lines.

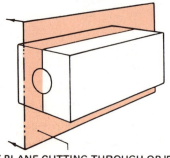

(A) IMAGINARY PLANE CUTTING THROUGH OBJECT

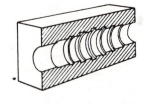

(B) CUTTING PLANE AND FRONT PORTION OF OBJECT REMOVED

FIGURE 23-1 CUTTING PLANE AND ITS APPLICATION

To obtain a sectional view, an imaginary cutting plane is passed through the object as shown in figure 23-1A. Figure 23-1B shows the front portion of the object removed. The direction and surface through which the cutting plane passes is represented on the drawing by a cutting plane line. The exposed surfaces, which have been cut through, are further identified by a number of slant lines called *section* or *cross-hatch* lines. If the cutting plane passes completely through the object, the sectional view is called a *full section.*

① ARROWS SHOW DIRECTION
② LETTERS IDENTIFY SECTION

FIGURE 23-2 THE CUTTING PLANE LINE

CUTTING PLANE LINES

The cutting plane line is a heavy line with one long and two short dashes as shown in figure 23-2. The line represents the edge of the cutting plane. The arrowheads on the ends of the cutting plane line show the direction in which the section is viewed. A letter is usually placed near each arrowhead to identify the section.

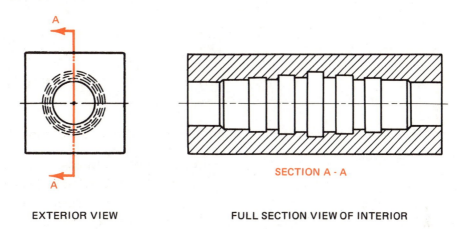

SECTION A - A

EXTERIOR VIEW   FULL SECTION VIEW OF INTERIOR

FIGURE 23-3 SECTION VIEWS SIMPLIFY INTERNAL DETAILS

CROSS-HATCHING OR SECTION LINING

The interpretation of a sectional drawing is simplified further by cross hatch or section lines, figure 23-3. It is easy to distinguish one part from another on a cutaway section (where section lines are used), because each combination of lightly drawn slant lines refers to a different material. The cross hatch line combinations are largely standardized and universally used so that they constantly refer to the same materials, figure 23-4.

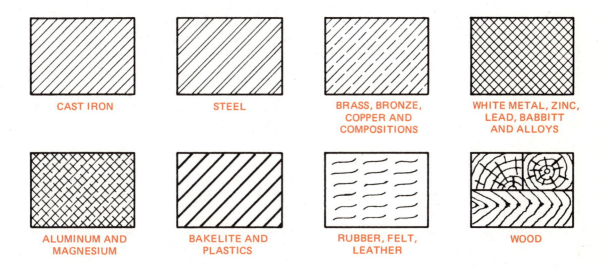

CAST IRON   STEEL   BRASS, BRONZE, COPPER AND COMPOSITIONS   WHITE METAL, ZINC, LEAD, BABBITT AND ALLOYS

ALUMINUM AND MAGNESIUM   BAKELITE AND PLASTICS   RUBBER, FELT, LEATHER   WOOD

FIGURE 23-4 SECTION LININGS IDENTIFY MATERIALS

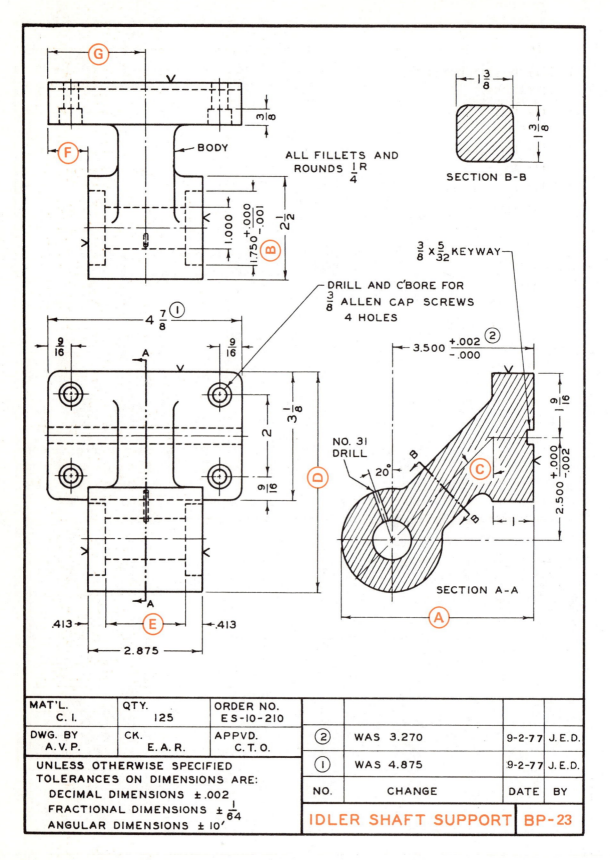

SECTION B-B

ALL FILLETS AND
ROUNDS $\frac{1}{4}$ R

BODY

$\frac{3}{8}$ × $\frac{5}{32}$ KEYWAY

DRILL AND C'BORE FOR
$\frac{3}{8}$ ALLEN CAP SCREWS
4 HOLES

NO. 31
DRILL

SECTION A-A

MAT'L. C.I.	QTY. 125	ORDER NO. ES-10-210				
DWG. BY A.V.P.	CK. E.A.R.	APPVD. C.T.O.	②	WAS 3.270	9-2-77	J.E.D.
UNLESS OTHERWISE SPECIFIED TOLERANCES ON DIMENSIONS ARE:			①	WAS 4.875	9-2-77	J.E.D.
DECIMAL DIMENSIONS ±.002			NO.	CHANGE	DATE	BY
FRACTIONAL DIMENSIONS ± $\frac{1}{64}$ ANGULAR DIMENSIONS ± 10'			IDLER SHAFT SUPPORT		BP-23	

IDLER SHAFT SUPPORT (BP-23)

1. Give the specifications for the counterbored holes.

2. How deep is the counterbored portion of the holes?

3. Give the specifications for the flat keyway.

4. What size are the fillets and rounds?

5. What size drill is used for the hole drilled at an angle?

6. Give the tolerance on the 20° dimension.

7. Compute angle Ⓒ from dimensions given on the drawing.

8. Give the maximum diameter for the 1″ hole.

9. What is the largest size to which diameter Ⓑ can be bored?

10. How are the machined surfaces indicated?

11. What type line shows where Section A-A is taken? In what view?

12. Determine dimensions Ⓐ and Ⓓ.

13. Determine from Section B-B what material is required.

14. How wide and thick is the body?

15. Indicate what two changes were made from the original drawing.

16. Determine minimum dimension Ⓔ.

17. Compute maximum dimension Ⓕ.

18. What is upper limit of dimension Ⓖ?

19. Why is section A-A a full section?

20. Show the section linings for aluminum and for steel.

21. Identify (a) the system of dimensioning and (b) the classification of tolerances.

22. Change the tolerances as follows: Decimal $\begin{array}{c}+.003''\\-.000''\end{array}$ Fractional $\begin{array}{c}+\frac{1}{64}''\\-0''\end{array}$ Angular $\begin{array}{c}+10'\\-0'\end{array}$

Then, compute the upper and lower limit for angle Ⓒ and dimensions Ⓐ Ⓓ Ⓔ Ⓕ and Ⓖ.

ASSIGNMENT   UNIT 23

Student's Name _____

1. _____

2. _____

3. _____

4. _____ 5. _____

6. _____ 7. Ⓒ = _____

8. _____ 9. _____

10. _____

11. _____

12. Ⓐ = _____ Ⓓ = _____

13. _____

14. _____

15. _____

16. Ⓔ = _____

17. Ⓕ = _____

18. Ⓖ = _____

19. _____

20.
Aluminum [ ]   Steel [ ]

21. (a) _____

(b) _____

22. Angle Ⓒ = _____

Ⓐ = _____

Ⓓ = _____

Ⓔ = _____

Ⓕ = _____

Ⓖ = _____

HALF SECTIONS, PARTIAL SECTIONS AND CONVENTIONAL BREAKS

HALF SECTIONS

The internal and external details of a part may be represented clearly by a sectional view called a *half section.* In a half section view, one half of the object is drawn in section and the other half is drawn as an exterior view, figure 24-1. The half section is used principally where both the inside and outside details are symmetrical and where a full section would omit some important detail in an exterior view.

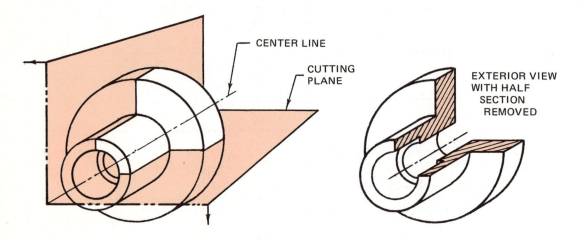

FIGURE 24-1 HALF-SECTION VIEW

Theoretically, the cutting plane for a half-section view extends halfway through the object, stopping at the axis or center line, figure 24-2. Drawings of simple symmetrical parts may not always include the cutting plane line or the arrows and letters showing the direction in which the section is taken. Also, hidden lines are not shown in the sectional view unless they are needed to give details of construction or for dimensioning.

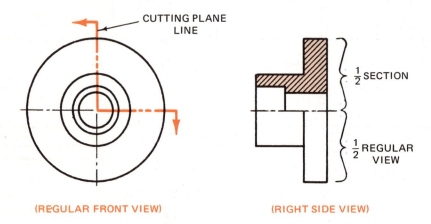

FIGURE 24-2 CUTTING PLANE LINE AND HALF SECTION VIEW

BROKEN OR PARTIAL SECTIONS

On some parts, it is not necessary to use either a full or a half section to expose the interior details. In such cases, a *broken-out* or *partial section* may be used, figure 24-3. The cutting plane is imagined as being passed through a portion of the object and the part in front of the plane is then broken away. The break line is an irregular freehand line which separates the internal sectioned view and the external view.

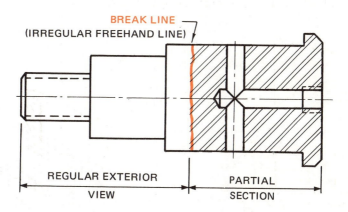

FIGURE 24-3 EXAMPLE OF A BROKEN-OUT OR PARTIAL SECTION

CONVENTIONAL BREAKS

A long part with a uniform cross section may be drawn to fit on a standard size drawing sheet by cutting out a portion of the length. In this manner, a part may be drawn larger to bring out some complicated details.

The cutaway portion may be represented by a conventional symbol which does two things: (1) it indicates that a portion of uniform cross section is removed, and (2) it shows the internal shape. A few conventional symbols which are accepted as standard are illustrated in figure 24-4.

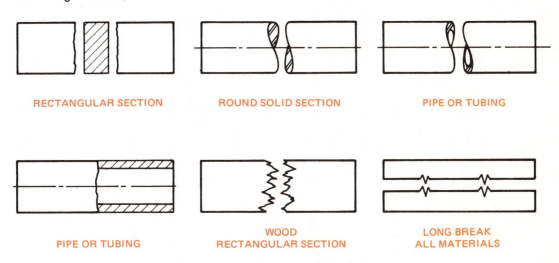

FIGURE 24-4 STANDARD BREAK SYMBOLS

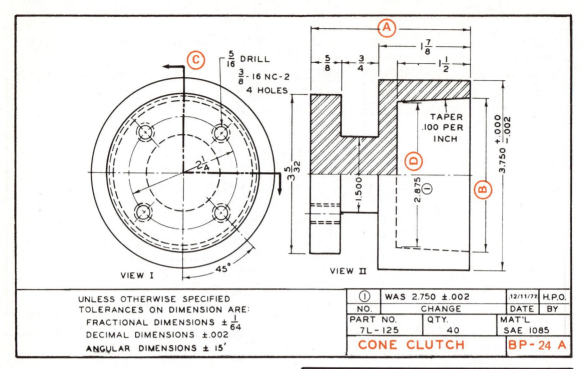

UNLESS OTHERWISE SPECIFIED
TOLERANCES ON DIMENSION ARE:
FRACTIONAL DIMENSIONS ± $\frac{1}{64}$
DECIMAL DIMENSIONS ±.002
ANGULAR DIMENSIONS ± 15'

①	WAS 2.750 ±.002	12/11/77	H.P.O.
NO.	CHANGE	DATE	BY
PART NO. 7L-125	QTY. 40	MAT'L SAE 1085	
CONE CLUTCH		**BP-24 A**	

CONE CLUTCH (BP-24A)

1. Name View I and View II.

2. What type line is Ⓒ ?

3. Give the specifications for the tapped holes.

4. What type of screw thread representation is used?

5. On what diameter are the threaded holes located?

6. Give the upper limit dimension for the 45° angle.

7. Determine overall width Ⓐ .

8. Give lower limit for the 1.500'' DIA.

9. Compute dimension Ⓑ .

10. Give the original diameter of Ⓓ .

11. Change the tolerances as follows:

Fractional dimensions $^{+0}_{-\frac{1}{64}}$'' Decimal dimensions $^{+.000}_{-.0025}$'' Angular dimensions $^{+5'}_{-15'}$

Then, compute the upper and lower limits for the 45° angle and dimensions Ⓐ, Ⓑ, and Ⓓ.

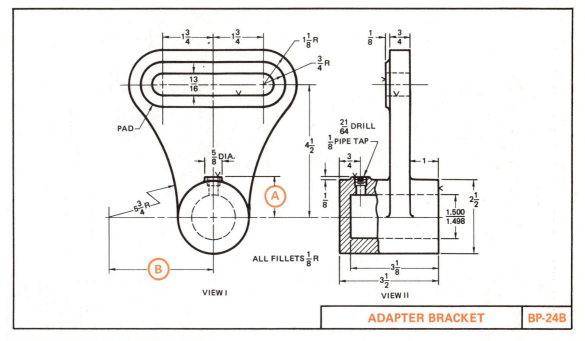

ADAPTER BRACKET   BP-24B

ADAPTER BRACKET (BP-24B)

1. Name View I and View II.
2. How many outside machined surfaces are indicated in View II?
3. Give the upper and lower limits of the bored hole.
4. How deep is the hole bored?
5. What is the drill size for the tapped hole?
6. What size pipe tap is used?
7. Give the center-to-center distance of the elongated slot.
8. Compute dimension Ⓐ.
9. Determine overall length of pad.
10. Compute dimension Ⓑ.
11. Add a $\begin{smallmatrix} +\ \frac{1''}{64} \\ -\ 0 \end{smallmatrix}$ tolerance to all fractional dimensions. Then, determine the upper and lower limit dimensions for;
   a. The depth of the bored hole.
   b. The center-to-center distance between the elongated slot and the bored hole.
   c. The overall width of the bracket (View I).
   d. The overall bracket length.
   e. Dimensions Ⓐ and Ⓑ.

ASSIGNMENT B UNIT 24

Student's Name _____

1. (I) _____
   (II) _____
2. _____
3. Upper _____
   Lower _____
4. _____
5. _____
6. _____
7. _____
8. Ⓐ = _____
9. _____
10. Ⓑ = _____
11. (a) Min. _____ Max. _____
    (b) Min. _____ Max. _____
    (c) Min. _____ Max. _____
    (d) Min. _____ Max. _____
    (e) A Min. _____ Max. _____
       Min. _____ Max. _____

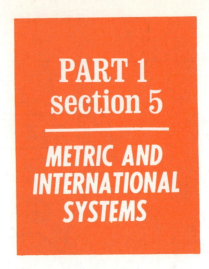

UNIT 25 — *METRIC SYSTEM DIMENSIONING, DIAMETRAL DIMENSIONS, AND ISO SYMBOLS*

The International System of Units (SI) was established by agreement among many nations to provide a logical interconnected framework for all measurements used in industry, science, and commerce. *SI* is a modernized version of the Metric system and relates to six basic units of measurement: (1) length, (2) time, (3) mass, (4) temperature, (5) electric current, and (6) luminous intensity. Multiples and submultiples of these basic units are expressed in decimals. All additional SI units are derived from the six basic units.

THE METRIC SYSTEM OF MEASUREMENT

The Metric·system of measurement is gaining wide acceptance by industry, throughout America and the world. The system has been used by the chemical and photographic industries, the medical professions, and in other areas for many years. As the use of the system spreads, dimensions and other features on drawings will gradually change to units of measurement expressed as metric units or as a combination of both the Metric and the International systems.

Prefixes are used in the Metric system to show how the dimension relates to a basic unit. For example, *deci-* means one-tenth of the basic unit of measure. Thus, 1 decimeter = 0.1 of a meter; 1 deciliter = 0.1 liter; and 1 decigram = 0.1 gram. Similarly, *centi-* = one hundredth; and *milli-* = one thousandth.

Dimensions larger than the basic unit of measure are expressed with the following prefixes: *deka-* = ten times greater; *hecto-* = one hundred times; and *kilo-* = 1,000 times greater. The most common unit of metric measure used on drawings is the millimeter (mm). The next frequently used unit is the meter (M).

CONVERTING METRIC AND INCH SYSTEM DIMENSIONS

Trade and engineering handbooks contain conversion charts which simplify the process of determining in one system the equivalent value of a dimension given in the other system. Sections of a conversion table are illustrated in figure 25-1 to show British inch units and equivalent metric units. Figure 25-1 also includes a drill series ranging from

#80 to #1, letter size drills from (A) to (Z), and fractional dimensions from .001″ to 1.000″. Note that millimeter equivalents, correct to four decimal places, are shown for both the drill sizes and the decimals which represent fractional parts of an inch.

The millimeter range of the table is from 0.0254 to 25.4000 mm, corresponding to 0.001″ to 1.000″, respectively. The millimeter equivalent of a measurement in the inch system may be found by multiplying the decimal value by 25.40.

Drill No. or Letter		Inch	mm
		.001	0.0254
		.002	0.0508
		.003	0.0762
		.004	0.1016
		.005	0.1270
		.006	0.1524
		.007	0.1778
		.008	0.2032
		.009	0.2286
		.010	0.2540
		.011	0.2794
		.012	0.3048
80	.0135	.013	0.3302
79	.0145	.014	0.3556
		.015	0.3810
	1/64	.0156	0.3969
78		.016	0.4064
		.017	0.4318
77		.018	0.4572
		.019	0.4826
76		.020	0.5080
75		.021	0.5334
74	.0225	.022	0.5588
		.023	0.5842
73		.024	0.6096

Drill No. or Letter		Inch	mm
		.401	10.1854
		.402	10.2108
		.403	10.2362
Y		.404	10.2616
		.405	10.2870
		.406	10.3124
13/32		.4062	10.3187
		.407	10.3378
		.408	10.3632
		.409	10.3886
		.410	10.4140
		.411	10.4394
		.412	10.4648
Z		.413	10.4902
		.414	10.5156
		.415	10.5410
		.416	10.5664
		.417	10.5918
		.418	10.6172
		.419	10.6426
		.420	10.6680
		.421	10.6934
27/64		.4219	10.7156
		.422	10.7188
		.423	10.7442

Drill No. or Letter		Inch	mm
		.220	5.5880
2		.221	5.6134
		.222	5.6388
		.223	5.6642
		.224	5.6896
		.225	5.7150
		.226	5.7404
		.227	5.7658
1		.228	5.7912
		.229	5.8166
		.230	5.8420
		.231	5.8674
		.232	5.8928
		.233	5.9182
A		.234	5.9436
	15/64	.2344	5.9531
		.235	5.9690
		.236	5.9944
		.2362	6.0000
		.237	6.0198
B		.238	6.0452
		.239	6.0706
		.240	6.0960
		.241	6.1214

Drill No. or Letter		Inch	mm
		.980	24.8920
		.981	24.9174
		.982	24.9428
		.983	24.9682
		.984	24.9936
		.9843	25.0000
63/64		.9844	25.0031
		.985	25.0190
		.986	25.0444
		.987	25.0698
		.988	25.0952
		.989	25.1206
		.990	25.1460
		.991	25.1714
		.992	25.1968
		.993	25.2222
		.994	25.2476
		.995	25.2730
		.996	25.2984
		.997	25.3238
		.998	25.3492
		.999	25.3746
		1.000	25.4000

FIGURE 25-1 PORTIONS OF A CONVERSION TABLE SHOWING DRILL SIZES AND mm EQUIVALENTS TO INCH DIMENSIONS

ROUNDING-OFF LINEAR DIMENSIONS

Many dimensions that are converted from inches to millimeters or from millimeters to inches are rounded-off. With 1 mm = 0.03937″, conversions can be made to very high limits of accuracy. This is done by calculating the decimal value to a greater number of digits than is required within the range of tolerances.

Production costs are related directly to the degree of accuracy required to produce a part. Therefore, the limits of dimensions should be rounded off to the least number of digits in the decimal dimension which will provide the greatest tolerance and ensure interchangeability.

A decimal dimension may be rounded off by increasing the last required digit by (1) if the digit which follows on the right is (5) or greater or by leaving the last digit unchanged if the digit to the right is less than (5).

For example, 1.5875″   rounded off to three decimal places = 1.588″
1.5874 mm rounded off to three decimal places = 1.587 mm
1.646 mm   rounded off to two decimal places   = 1.65 mm
1.644″   rounded off to two decimal places   = 1.64″

DIAMETRAL DIMENSIONS

The symbol ∅ on a drawing shows that the part has cylindrical sections. For example, a gear blank may be fully described in one view by using the diametral dimension symbol ∅ to indicate the cylindrical surfaces. The one-view drawing shows a gear blank with a 6.024″ outside diameter (= 153 mm), 1.250″ bore (= 31.75 mm), and 1.024″ thickness (= 26 mm). Note that the dimensions of the outside diameter and the bore are followed by the symbol ∅ .

While figure 25-2 gives the dimensions in the Metric system, they could be shown in either system or by a combination of both systems.

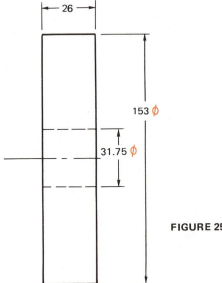

FIGURE 25-2 USE OF DIAMETRAL
DIMENSION SYMBOL

PROJECTION SYMBOLS

The International Organization for Standardization (ISO) recommends the use of a projection symbol on drawings that are produced in one country for use among many countries, figure 25-3. The projection symbols are intended to promote the accurate exchange of technical information through drawings.

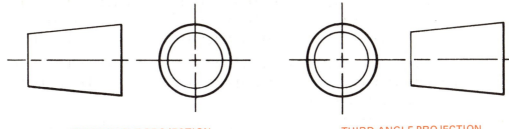

FIRST ANGLE PROJECTION   THIRD ANGLE PROJECTION

FIGURE 25-3 ISO PROJECTION SYMBOLS (ENLARGED)

The United States and Canada use the third-angle system of projection for drawings. Other countries, however, use a different system which is known as the first-angle projection system. The purpose of introducing the ISO projection symbols is to indicate that there is a continuously increasing international exchange of drawings for the production of interchangeable parts. Thus, the symbol tells whether the drawing follows the third-angle or the first-angle projection system.

The ISO projection symbol, the notation on tolerances, and information on whether metric and/or inch dimensions are used on the drawing should appear as notes either within the title block or adjacent to it, figure 25-4.

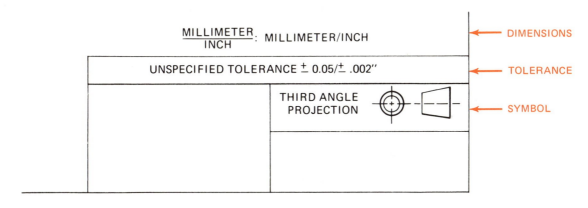

FIGURE 25-4 DIMENSION, TOLERANCE, AND SYMBOL NOTES IN A TITLE BLOCK

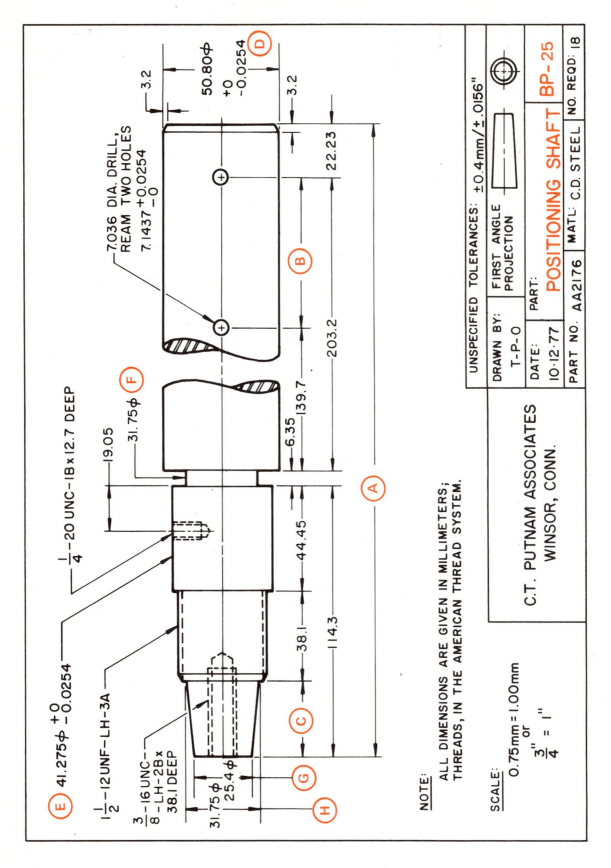

NOTE:

ALL DIMENSIONS ARE GIVEN IN MILLIMETERS;
THREADS, IN THE AMERICAN THREAD SYSTEM.

SCALE:

0.75mm = 1.00mm
or
$\frac{3''}{4} = 1''$

UNSPECIFIED TOLERANCES:	±0.4mm/±.0156"	
DRAWN BY: T-P-O	FIRST ANGLE PROJECTION	
DATE: 10·12·77	PART: POSITIONING SHAFT	BP-25
PART NO. AA2176	MATL: C.D. STEEL	NO. REQD: 18

C.T. PUTNAM ASSOCIATES
WINSOR, CONN.

50.80ϕ $^{+0}_{-0.0254}$

7.036 DIA. DRILL,
REAM TWO HOLES
7.1437 $^{+0.0254}_{-0}$

3.2

3.2

22.23

203.2

139.7

6.35

44.45

114.3

38.1

31.75ϕ

19.05

$1\frac{1}{4}$–20 UNC–1B×12.7 DEEP

E 41.275ϕ $^{+0}_{-0.0254}$

$1\frac{1}{2}$–12UNF–LH–3A

$\frac{3}{8}$–16 UNC–
–LH–2B×
38.1 DEEP

31.75ϕ

25.4ϕ

A B C D F G H

POSITIONING SHAFT (BP-25)

1. State what system of projection is used.
2. Indicate what unit of measurement is used for dimensioning.
3. Give the tolerance that applies on (a) metric dimensions and (b) dimensions converted to the inch system, when no tolerance is specified.
4. Compute the basic metric dimension for overall length (A) rounded off to two decimal places.
5. Determine the basic center-to-center distance between the two reamed holes (B), in millimeters.
6. Find the length of the tapered portion (C).
7. Determine the equivalent British (inch) units for each linear dimension, rounded off to two decimal places. Use a four-place millimeter/inch conversion chart, if available.
8. Convert each metric diametral dimension to its equivalent inch dimension, correct to three decimal places.
9. Give the letter size drill which corresponds to the drill size of the two reamed holes.
10. State what system of representation is used for the threaded sections.
11. Convert the depth of each tapped hole to its equivalent in the inch system.
12. Tell what each part of the three thread dimensions designates.
13. Give the minimum and maximum limits of diametral dimensions (D) and (E) in metric and inch dimensions, correct to three decimal places.
14. Determine the minimum and maximum limits of diametral dimensions (F), (G), and (H), rounded to two decimal places.
15. Determine the (a) taper per foot of the tapered portion, correct to two decimal places, and (b) convert the taper per foot to its millimeter equivalent.
16. Compute the lower and upper dimensional limits of each linear dimension in both the metric and inch systems. Round off the dimensions to two decimal places.

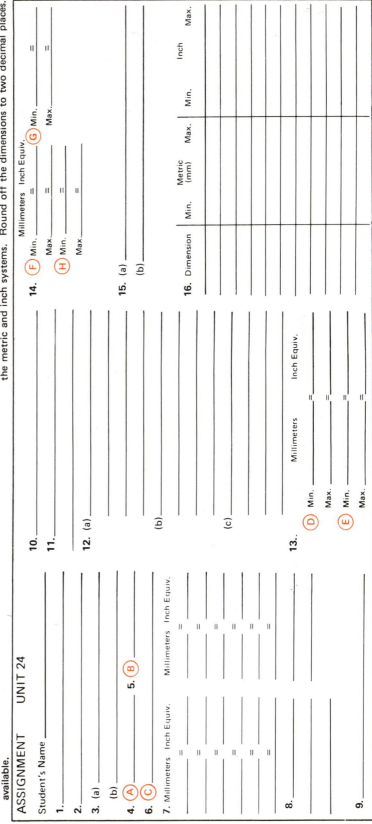

ASSIGNMENT   UNIT 24

Student's Name _____

1. _____
2. _____
3. (a) _____
   (b) _____
4. (A) _____
5. (B) _____
6. (C) _____
7. Millimeters Inch Equiv.   Millimeters Inch Equiv.
   ___ = ___   ___ = ___
   ___ = ___   ___ = ___
   ___ = ___   ___ = ___
   ___ = ___
8. _____
   Millimeters Inch Equiv.
13. (D) Min. ___ = ___
       Max. ___ = ___
    (E) Min. ___ = ___
       Max. ___ = ___
9. _____

10. _____
11. _____
12. (a) _____
    (b) _____
    (c) _____
14. (F) Min. ___ = ___
       Max. ___ = ___
    (H) Min. ___ = ___
       Max. ___ = ___
    (G) Min. ___ = ___
       Max. ___ = ___
15. (a) _____
    (b) _____

16.

Dimension	Metric (mm)		Inch	
	Min.	Max.	Min.	Max.

107

PROJECTION BASED ON SYSTEM OF QUADRANTS

The position each view of an object occupies, as treated thus far in this text, is based upon the United States and Canadian standard of third-angle projection. Third-angle projection is derived from a theoretical division of all space into four quadrants. The horizontal plane in figure 26-1 represents an X-axis. The vertical plane is the Y-axis. The four quadrants produced by the two planes are shown as I, II, III, and IV.

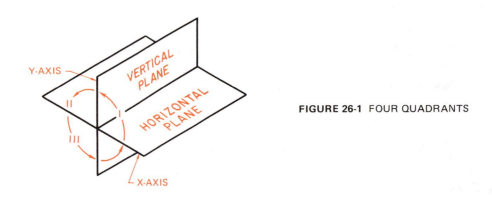

FIGURE 26-1 FOUR QUADRANTS

It is possible to place an object in any one of the four quadrants. Views of the object may then be projected. The third quadrant was adopted in the United States and Canada because the projected views of an object occupy a natural position. Drawings produced by such standards of projection are comparatively easy to interpret. Each view is projected so the object is represented as it is seen. The principles of third-angle projection are reviewed graphically in figure 26-2.

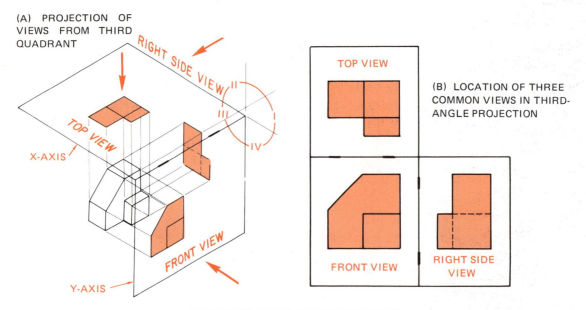

(A) PROJECTION OF VIEWS FROM THIRD QUADRANT

(B) LOCATION OF THREE COMMON VIEWS IN THIRD-ANGLE PROJECTION

FIGURE 26-2 THIRD-ANGLE PROJECTION

METRIC: FIRST-ANGLE PROJECTION

Increasing worldwide commerce and the interchange of materials, instruments, machine tools, and other precision-made parts and mechanisms require the interpretation of drawings which have been prepared according to different systems of projection. The accepted standard of projection of the Common Market and other countries of the world relates to the first quadrant (I). The system, therefore, is identified as *first-angle projection.*

Dimensions given in the metric system are used with first-angle drawings. As world leaders in business and industry, the United States and Canada are also using a great number of first-angle projection drawings.

The quadrants and X and Y axes in first-angle projection are shown in figure 26-3. Arrows are used in figure 26-3 (A) to illustrate positions from which the object in quadrant I may be viewed. The three common views are named Front View, Top View, and Left-Side View. These views are positioned in figure 26-3 (B) as they would appear (without the imaginary projection box outline) on a drawing.

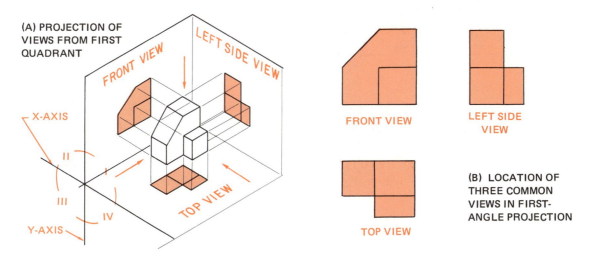

FIGURE 26-3 FIRST-ANGLE PROJECTION SHOWING POSITION OF VIEWS

In contrast with third-angle projection, the top view in first-angle projection appears under the front view. Similarly, the left-side view is drawn in the position occupied by the right-side- view in third-angle projection. This positioning, which is not natural, makes it more difficult to visualize and interpret first-angle drawings. Each view in first-angle projection is projected through the object from a surface of the object to the corresponding projection plane. However, the views in both first-angle and third-angle projection provide essential information for the craftsperson to produce or assemble a single part of a complete mechanism.

DIMENSIONING FIRST-ANGLE DRAWINGS

Dimensions on first-angle drawings are in Metric. When a numerical value is less than 1, the first numeral is preceded by a zero and a decimal point. For example, the decimal .733 is dimensioned to read 0.733. Certain countries of Europe use a comma in the place of a decimal point. In this case the decimal .733 is dimensioned to read 0,733. This value is followed by the unit of measurement, like mm, to read 0,733 mm.

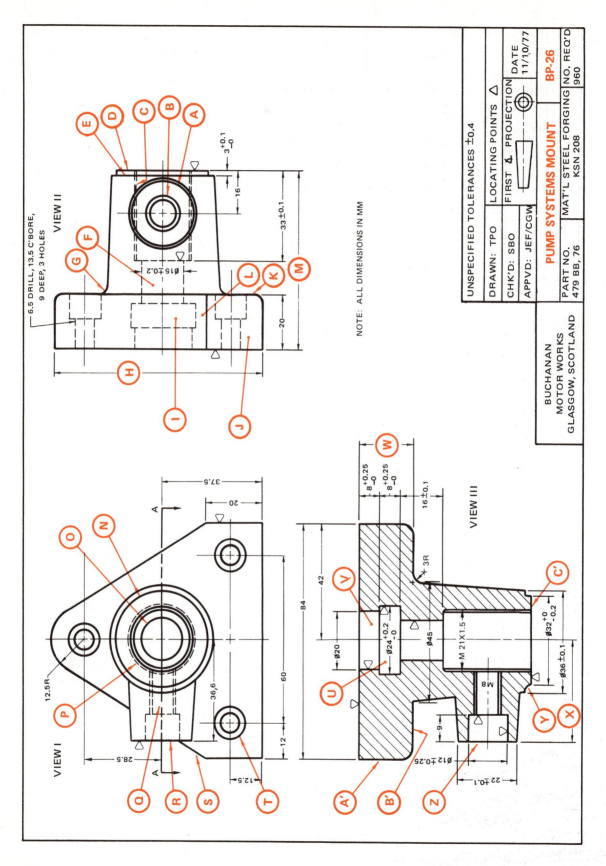

PUMP SYSTEMS MOUNT (BP-26)

1. State what system of projection is used.

2. Name views I, II, and III.

3. Give the symbol which indicates a diameter.

4. Tell what the symbol △ indicates.

5. State what the comma denotes in the 36,6 dimension.

6. Indicate what tolerance to use if none is given.

7. Give the specifications for the counter-bored holes 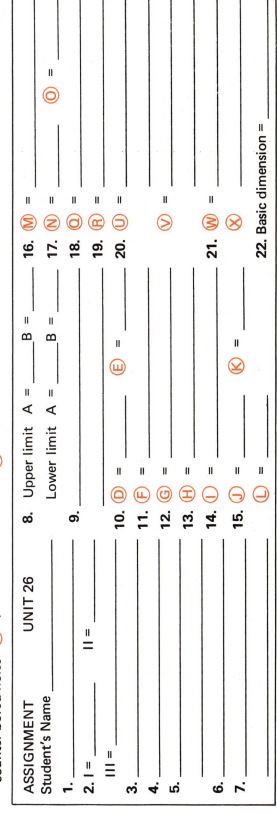T .

8. Determine the upper and lower limit dimensions for diameters Ⓐ and Ⓑ .

9. Give the ISO designation for threads Ⓒ . Describe what each value means.

10. Locate surfaces Ⓓ and Ⓔ in view III.

11. State the minimum diameter for hole Ⓕ .

12. Give the radius of fillet Ⓖ .

13. Compute maximum overall dimension Ⓗ .

14. Give the minimum width of undercut Ⓘ .

15. Locate surfaces Ⓙ and surface Ⓛ in view III and surface Ⓛ in view I.

16. Compute maximum overall dimension Ⓜ , adding all the + tolerances to the basic dimensions.

17. Give minimum diameters Ⓝ and Ⓞ .

18. State the thread size for Ⓠ .

19. Locate surface Ⓡ in view III.

20. Give the minimum diameter and width of holes Ⓤ and Ⓥ .

21. Determine maximum overall dimensions Ⓦ and Ⓧ .

22. Determine the basic dimension between surfaces Ⓔ and Ⓚ .

ASSIGNMENT   UNIT 26

Student's Name _____

1. _____

2. I = _____   II = _____

III = _____

3. _____

4. _____

5. _____

6. _____

7. _____

8. Upper limit A = _____ B = _____

Lower limit A = _____ B = _____

9. _____

10. Ⓓ = _____ Ⓔ = _____

11. Ⓕ = _____

12. Ⓖ = _____

13. Ⓗ = _____

14. Ⓘ = _____

15. Ⓙ = _____ Ⓚ = _____

Ⓛ = _____

16. Ⓜ = _____

17. Ⓝ = _____

18. Ⓠ = _____

19. Ⓡ = _____

20. Ⓤ = _____

Ⓥ = _____

21. Ⓦ = _____

Ⓧ = _____

22. Basic dimension = _____

111

DUAL SYSTEMS OF SCREW THREADS, DIMENSIONING, AND TOLERANCES

SCREW THREAD CONVERSION

A dual system of screw threads will exist for many years until the advantages of the *Unified Inch* system of America, Britain, and Canada are combined with those of the International Organization for Standardization of Metric Thread Series (ISO) to produce a single new International Standard Screw Thread System.

In the meantime, screw threads may be designated either by the present American Unified thread sizes or by Metric ISO sizes. The Metric thread series ranges from .30 UNM *(Unified Metric)* to 1.40 UNM, and from M1.6 (with a pitch of 0.35 millimeters) to M39 X 2. The M39 X 2 ISO designation indicates that the thread has an outside diameter of 39 millimeters and a thread pitch of 2 millimeters.

Screw thread conversion tables usually contain engineering data on the outside diameter and pitch for ISO designated numbers, the present American Unified thread sizes, and the best Metric equivalent for certain American thread sizes.

For example, a 1/2-20 UNF designation on a drawing indicates that the outside diameter of the thread is .500'' (for the 1/2'') and the pitch is 20 threads per inch. Although there is no current precise metric equivalent, the outside diameter and pitch, expressed in metric units is 12.7 mm O.D. and 1.27 mm pitch.

The threads illustrated on the tap and by the drawing of a similarly threaded hole are dual dimensioned as shown in figure 27-1.

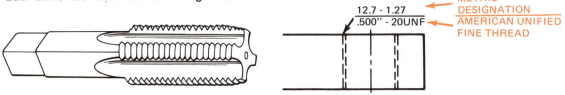

FIGURE 27-1 DUAL DIMENSIONING A TAPPED HOLE

CONTROLLING DIMENSIONS

The usual designation for millimeter dimensions on a drawing is mm and for meters, M. If all dimensions are in the Metric system, the drawing usually carries a note to indicate what unit of measurement or scale is used.

When a drawing contains dimensions in both the inch and the Metric systems, the dimension in which the product was designed *(controlling dimension)* appears above the dimension line. The converted value appears below the line, figure 27-2.

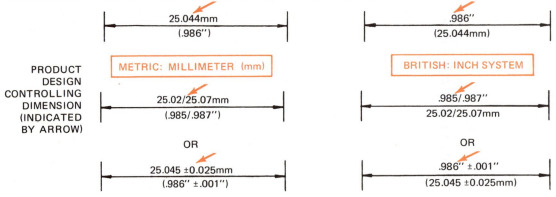

FIGURE 27-2 CONTROLLING DIMENSIONS

DUAL DIMENSIONING

As industry changes gradually from the English to the Metric system, it will be necessary to use *dual dimensioning.* When parts are dual-dimensioned, it means that the parts may be produced in any country regardless of whether the English system inch dimensions or Metric dimensions, or both, are used. Dual dimensioning implies that each dimension is given both in Metric and English units. The Metric dimension (including tolerances) is given on one side of the dimension line; the inch dimension is given on the opposite side of the line. For example, if dual dimensioning is used on a dimension of 83 millimeters (or 3.268") the dimension is shown as,

If a tolerance of ±0.2 mm applies to the base dimension of 83 mm, the dimension and tolerance in the English system equals 3.268" ± .008". The dual dimension is represented as,

Instead of a dimension line between the dimensions in the two systems, some industries use the slash (/) symbol between the Metric and British units for dual dimensioning.

$$\vdash\!\!-\!\!-\ 83 \pm 0.2 \text{MM}\ 3.268'' \pm .008''\ -\!\!-\!\!\dashv$$

UNILATERAL AND EQUAL/UNEQUAL BILATERAL TOLERANCES

The previous examples showed equal tolerances in both directions (±). However, some tolerances may be unequal or unilateral. If unequal bilateral tolerances of $^{+0.2}_{-0.1}$ mm are applied to the 83 mm dimension, the drawing (with the scale and dimensional systems indicated) is dimensioned as,

NONSIGNIFICANT ZEROS

A *nonsignificant zero* refers to a zero that has no value in a number other than to simplify reading of a dimension and to help in correctly interpreting the dimension. Drawings with dimensions in the English (inch) system contain nonsignificant zeros to the right of the decimal point so that both the dimension and the tolerance have the same number of digits.

Example: 3.7222" ± .0010

By contrast, nonsignificant zeros are *not* added to a decimal value in the Metric system. Thus, the number of digits in the base dimension and the tolerance may or may not be the same. For instance, the dimension and tolerance 72.5 ± 0.125 mm shows one digit in the fractional part of the base dimension (.5 mm), and three digits (0.125) for the bilateral decimal tolerance. A dimension that is less than one millimeter has a zero preceding the fractional value: like 0.90 mm.

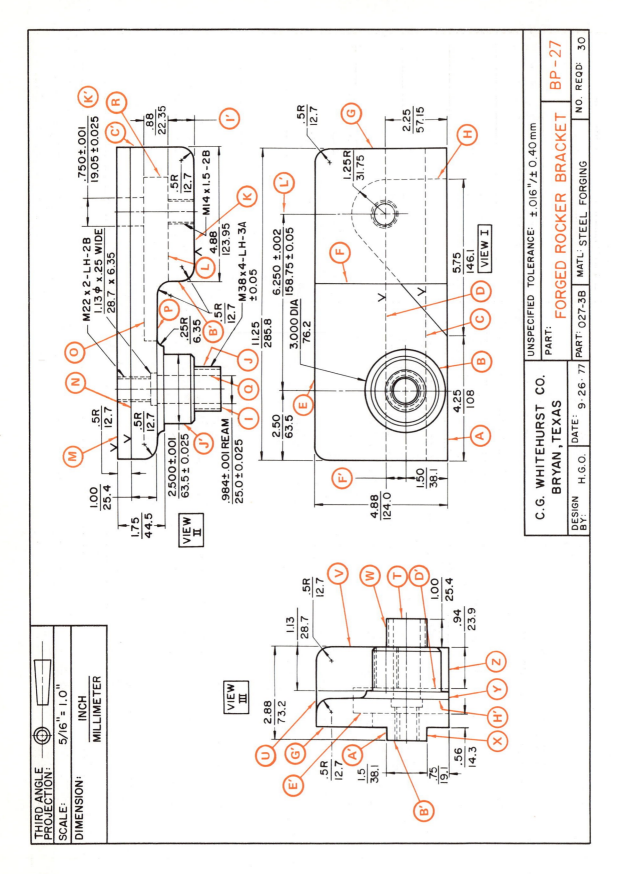

FORGED ROCKER BRACKET (BP-27)

1. Assume View I is the front view. Name Views II and III.

2. Name the dimensions above the line if these represent the product design dimensions.

3. State what dual dimensioning implies.

4. Determine what system of dimensioning is used.

5. Locate surfaces (A), (C), and (D) and (E) in View III. Give the corresponding letter.

6. Give the letters in View II that identify surfaces (F), (G) and (H).

7. Locate surfaces (I), (J), (K), (L), (M), (N), (O) and (P) in View III.

8. Determine the distance between the center of the .750″ hole and surface (G) correct to two decimal places. Give the dimension in Metric and British units.

9. Give the center distance (F′) in millimeters and inches, correct to two decimal places.

10. Locate thickness (I′) in both dimensioning systems, correct to one decimal place.

11. Indicate the tolerance to use if none is specified.

12. Interpret the meaning of the screw-thread designation M38X4-LH-3A.

13. Give the outside diameter and pitch (in millimeters) for each Metric screw thread.

14. Convert each Metric screw thread to its equivalent American screw thread.

15. Give the upper and lower dimensional limits of diameters (J) and (J′) in inch units, to three decimal places.

16. Determine the minimum and maximum metric dimensions for (K) and (L′), correct to three decimal places.

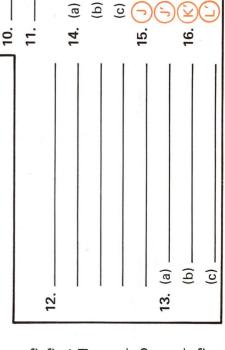

ASSIGNMENT   UNIT 25

Student's Name _____

1. _____
2. _____
3. _____
4. _____
5.   (A) = _____   (D) = _____
     (C) = _____   (E) = _____
6.   (F) = _____   (G) = _____   (H) = _____
7.   (I) = _____   (L) = _____   (O) = _____
     (J) = _____   (M) = _____   (P) = _____
     (K) = _____   (N) = _____
8. _____
9. _____
10. _____
11. _____
12. _____
13. (a) _____
     (b) _____
     (c) _____
14. (a) _____
     (b) _____
     (c) _____
15. (J) = _____
     (J′) = _____
16. (K′) = _____
     (L′) = _____

UNIT 28   *SKETCHING HORIZONTAL, VERTICAL, AND SLANT LINES*

THE VALUE OF SKETCHING

Many parts or assembled units may be described clearly and adequately by one or more freehand sketches. Sketching is another way of conveying ideas rather than a method of making perfect completed drawings.

Technicians, therefore, in addition to being able to interpret drawings and blueprints accurately and easily, are often required to make sketches. By sketching additional views not found on blueprints, a craftsperson can study the part thoroughly to understand the processes required to fabricate or machine it. Since the only tools needed are a soft pencil and any available paper, sketches may be made conveniently at any time or place.

SKETCHING LINES FREEHAND

The development of correct skills in sketching lines freehand is more essential for the beginner than speed. After the basic principles of sketching are learned and skill is acquired in making neat and accurate sketches, then stress should be placed on speed.

Although shop sketches are made on the job and special pencils are not required, a soft lead pencil with a cone-shaped point will produce the best results. For fine lines, use a fairly sharp point; for heavier lines, round the point more, figure 28-1.

FINE POINT – FINE LINE   BLUNT POINT – HEAVY LINE

FIGURE 28-1 SHARPNESS OF PENCIL POINT INFLUENCES LINE WEIGHT

SKETCHING HORIZONTAL LINES

The same principles of drafting which apply to the making of a mechanical drawing and the interpretation of blueprints are used for making sketches.

In sketching, the pencil is held 3/4" to 1" from the point so the lines to be drawn may be seen easily and there is a free and easy movement of the pencil. A free arm movement makes it possible to sketch smooth, neat lines as compared with the rough and inaccurate lines produced by a finger and wrist movement.

In planning the first horizontal line on a sketch, place two points on the paper to mark the beginning and end of the line, figure 28-2A. Place the pencil point on the first dot.

Then, with a free arm movement and with the eyes focused on the right point, draw the line from left to right, figure 28-2B.

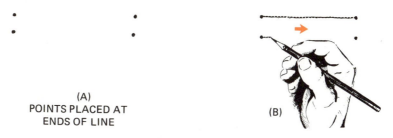

(A)
POINTS PLACED AT
ENDS OF LINE

(B)

FIGURE 28-2 SKETCHING HORIZONTAL LINES

Examine the line for straightness, smoothness, and weight. If the line is too light, a softer pencil or a more rounded point may be needed. On long lines, extra dots are often placed between the start and finish points of the line. These intermediate dots are used as a guide for drawing long straight lines.

SKETCHING VERTICAL LINES

The same techniques for holding the pencil and using a free arm movement apply in sketching vertical lines. Dots again may be used to indicate the beginning and end of the vertical line. Start the line from the top and move the pencil downward as shown in figure 28-3. For long lines, if possible, the paper may be turned to a convenient position.

FIGURE 28-3 SKETCHING VERTICAL LINES

FIGURE 28-4 SKETCHING SLANT LINES

SKETCHING SLANT LINES

The three types of straight lines which are widely used in drawing and sketching are: (1) horizontal, (2) vertical, and (3) inclined or slant lines.

The slant line may be drawn either from the top down or from the bottom up. The use of dots at the starting and stopping points for slant lines is helpful to the beginner. Slant lines, figure 28-4, are produced with the same free arm movement used for horizontal and vertical lines.

USING GRAPH PAPER

Many industries recommend the use of graph paper for making sketches. Graph paper is marked to show how many squares are included in each inch. The combination of light ruled lines at a fixed number per inch makes it possible to draw neat sketches which are fairly accurate in size. Throughout this text, squared or isometric graph sections are included for each sketching assignment. Other ruled section papers are available with diametric, oblique or perspective lines.

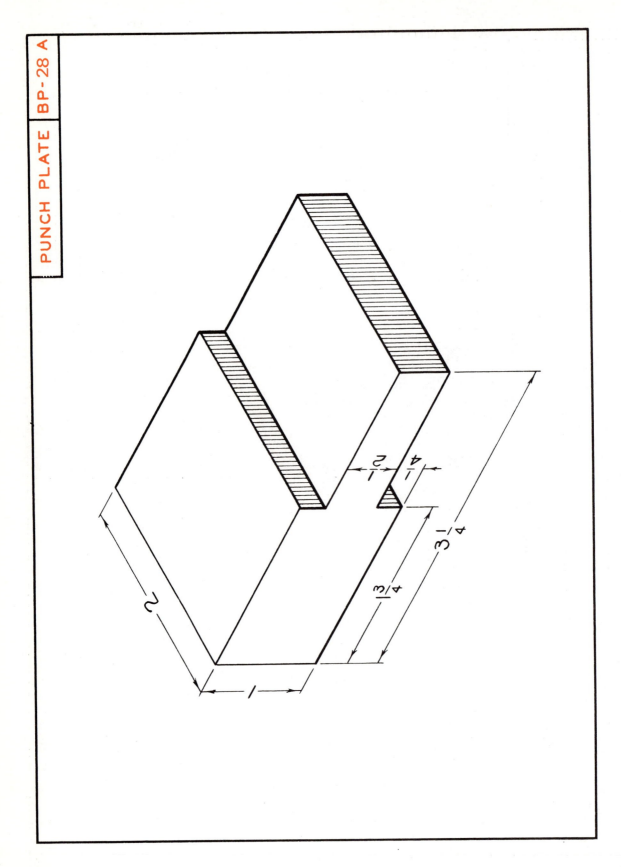

PUNCH PLATE | BP-28 A

ASSIGNMENT A   UNIT 28

STUDENT'S NAME _____

SUGGESTIONS

① START THE FRONT VIEW 1" FROM THE LEFT HAND
   MARGIN AND 1½" FROM THE BOTTOM

② ALLOW 1" BETWEEN THE VIEWS

SKETCHING ASSIGNMENT FOR PUNCH PLATE (BP- 28A)

① SKETCH THREE VIEWS: FRONT, TOP AND RIGHT SIDE

② DIMENSION EACH VIEW

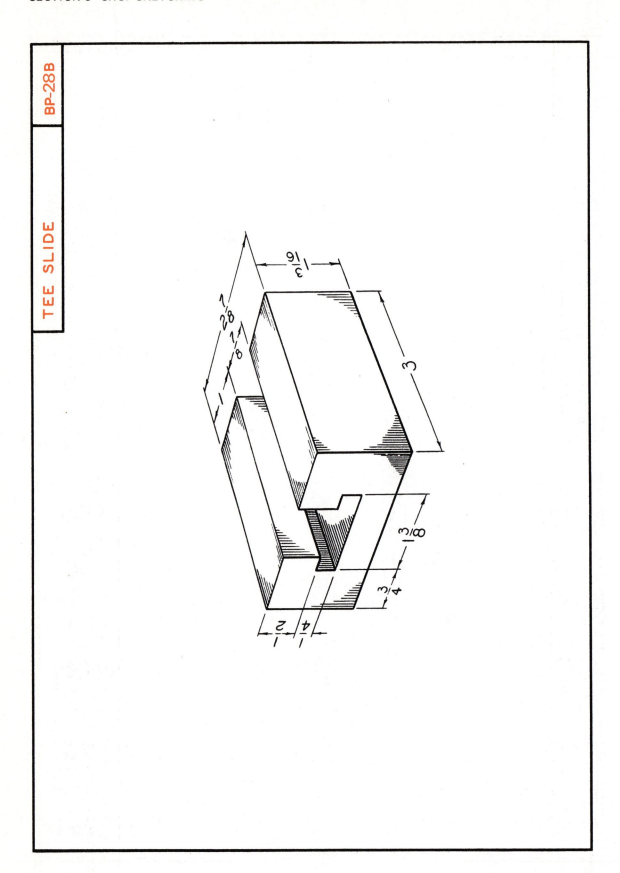

BP-28B

TEE SLIDE

ASSIGNMENT B   UNIT 28

STUDENT'S NAME _____

SKETCHING ASSIGNMENT FOR TEE SLIDE (BP-28 B)

① MAKE FREEHAND SKETCHES OF THE FRONT, TOP AND LEFT SIDE VIEWS

② DIMENSION THE VIEWS

SUGGESTIONS

① CENTER THE SKETCHES ON THE SQUARED SECTIONS

② ALLOW $\frac{3}{4}"$ BETWEEN THE VIEWS

UNIT 29   SKETCHING CURVED LINES AND CIRCLES

ARCS CONNECTING STRAIGHT LINES

Often, when describing a part, it is necessary to draw both straight and curved lines. When part of a circle is shown, the curved line is usually called an *arc.*

When an arc must be drawn so that it connects two straight lines (in other words, is tangent to them), it may be sketched easily if five basic steps are followed, figure 29-1.

STEP 1 ▶ Extend the straight lines so they intersect.

STEP 2 ▶ On the vertical and horizontal center lines, step off the same distance from the intersection (center) of both lines.

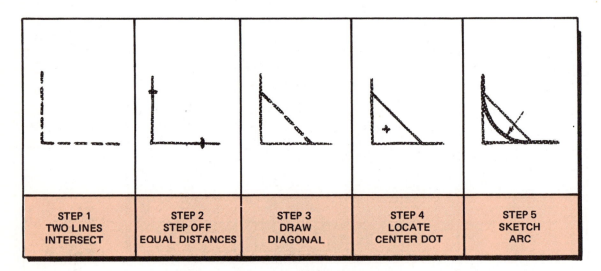

STEP 1 TWO LINES INTERSECT	STEP 2 STEP OFF EQUAL DISTANCES	STEP 3 DRAW DIAGONAL	STEP 4 LOCATE CENTER DOT	STEP 5 SKETCH ARC

FIGURE 29-1 SKETCHING AN ARC FREEHAND

STEP 3 ▶ Draw the diagonal line through these two points to form a triangle.

STEP 4 ▶ Place a dot in the center of the triangle.

STEP 5 ▶ Start at the vertical line and sketch an arc which runs through the dot and ends on the horizontal center line. Darken the arc and erase all unnecessary lines.

ARCS CONNECTING STRAIGHT AND CURVED LINES

Two other line combinations using straight lines and arcs are also very common. The first is the case of an arc connecting a straight line with another arc; the second is where an arc connects two other arcs. The same five basic steps are used as illustrated in figure 29-2.

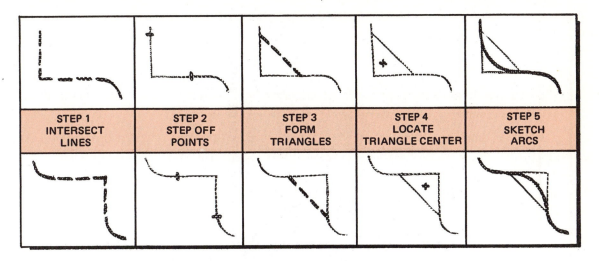

FIGURE 29-2 SKETCHING ARCS IN COMBINATION WITH OTHER ARCS

SKETCHING CIRCLES

Shop sketches also require the drawing of circles or parts of a circle. While there are many ways to draw a circle freehand, a well-formed circle can be sketched by following five simple steps which are described below and illustrated in figure 29-3.

STEP 1 ▶ Lay out the vertical and horizontal center lines in the correct location. Measure off half the diameter of the circle on each side of the two center lines.

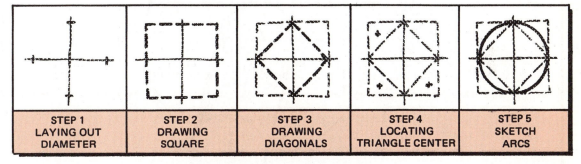

FIGURE 29-3 SKETCHING A CIRCLE

STEP 2 ▶ Draw lightly two vertical and two horizontal lines passing through the points marked off on the center lines. These lines, properly drawn, will be parallel and will form a square.

STEP 3 ▶ Draw diagonal lines from each corner of the square to form four triangles.

STEP 4 ▶ Place a dot in the center of each triangle through which an arc is to pass.

STEP 5 ▶ Sketch the arc for one quarter of the circle. Start at one center line and draw the arc through the dot to the next center line. Continue until the circle is complete. Darken the circle and erase all the guide lines to simplify the reading of the sketch.

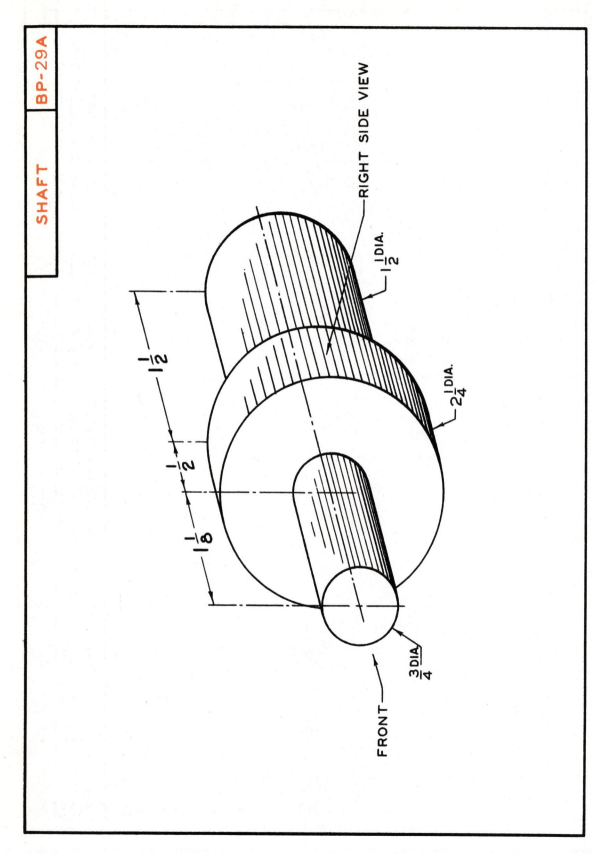

SHAFT

BP-29A

RIGHT SIDE VIEW

$1\frac{1}{2}$ DIA.

$2\frac{1}{4}$ DIA.

$\frac{3}{4}$ DIA.

FRONT

$1\frac{1}{2}$

$\frac{1}{2}$

$1\frac{1}{8}$

ASSIGNMENT A   UNIT 29

STUDENT'S NAME _____

SKETCHING ASSIGNMENT FOR SHAFT (BP-29A)

① SKETCH A FRONT AND RIGHT SIDE VIEW

② DIMENSION BOTH VIEWS

SUGGESTIONS

① DRAW VERTICAL CENTER LINE FOR FRONT VIEW 2" FROM LEFT BORDER

② DRAW HORIZONTAL CENTER LINE 2 3/4" FROM BOTTOM BORDER

③ ALLOW 1" BETWEEW VIEWS

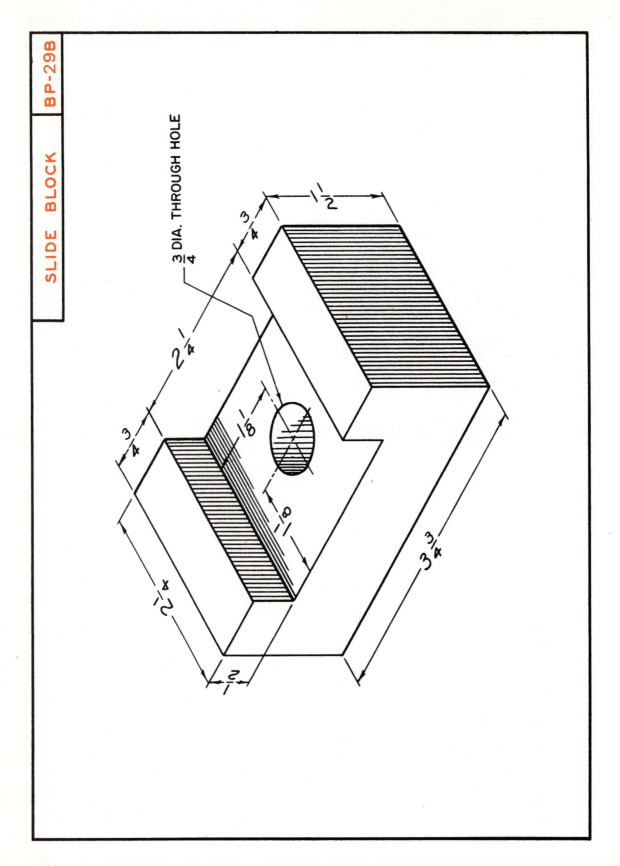

SLIDE BLOCK

BP-29B

$\frac{3}{4}$ DIA. THROUGH HOLE

ASSIGNMENT B   UNIT 29 _____

STUDENT'S NAME _____

SKETCHING ASSIGNMENT FOR SLIDE BLOCK (BP-29B)

① SKETCH THREE VIEWS: FRONT, TOP AND RIGHT SIDE

② DIMENSION EACH VIEW OF THE SKETCH

SUGGESTIONS

① START THE FRONT VIEW $\frac{5}{8}$" FROM THE LEFT HAND MARGIN AND $\frac{3}{8}$" FROM THE BOTTOM

② ALLOW $\frac{3}{4}$" BETWEEN THE VIEWS

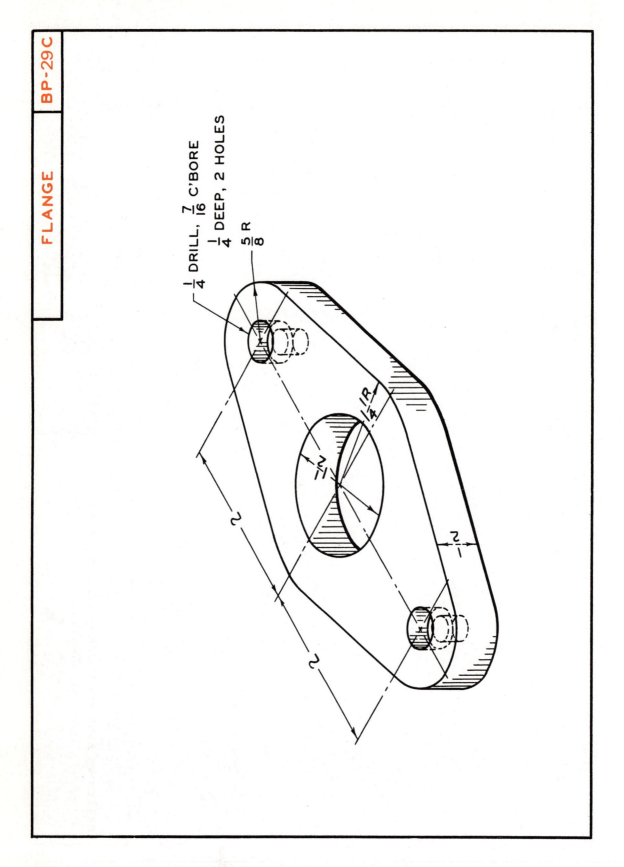

ASSIGNMENT C   UNIT 29

STUDENT'S NAME

SUGGESTIONS

① LAY OUT VERTICAL CENTER LINE SO THE SKETCH IS POSITIONED ON THE SHEET

② LAY OUT HORIZONTAL CENTER LINE FOR TOP VIEW

③ ALLOW 1" BETWEEN VIEWS

SKETCHING ASSIGNMENT FOR FLANGE (BP-29 C)

① MAKE A FREEHAND SKETCH OF THE TOP AND FRONT VIEWS

② DIMENSION THE VIEWS COMPLETELY

Parts that are irregular in shape often look complicated to sketch. However, the object may be drawn easily if it is first visualized as a series of square and rectangular blocks. Then, by using straight, slant, and curved lines in combination with each other, it is possible to draw in the squares and rectangles the exact shape of the part.

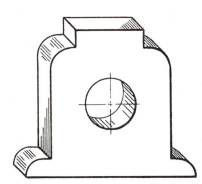

The Shaft Support shown in figure 30-1 is an example of a machine part that can be sketched easily by *blocking.* The support must first be thought of in terms of basic squares and rectangles. After these squares and rectangles are determined, the step-by-step procedures which are

FIGURE 30-1 EXAMPLE OF IRREGULARLY-SHAPED PART TO BE SKETCHED

commonly used to simplify the making of a sketch of an irregularly-shaped piece are applied. These step-by-step procedures are described next and their application is shown in figure 30-2.

STEP 1 ▶ Lay out the two basic rectangles required for the shaft support. Use light lines and draw the outline to the desired overall sketch size.

STEP 2 ▶ Place a dot at the center of the top horizontal line and draw the vertical center line. Also, draw two vertical lines for the sides of the top rectangle.

STEP 3 ▶ Locate dots and draw horizontal lines from the left vertical line to locate:

(a) The rectangle for the top of the support, and
(b) The center line of the hole.

STEP 4 ▶ Draw the squares for the rounded corners of the base, top, and the center hole. In these squares:

(a) Draw the diagonals and form the triangles, and
(b) Locate dots in the centers of the triangles through which each arc will pass.

STEP 5 ▶ Draw the arcs and circle. Start at one diagonal and draw the arc through the dot to the next diagonal. Continue until the circle is completed.

STEP 6 ▶ Draw the side view if necessary.

STEP 7 ▶ Darken all object lines and dimension. Erase those lines used in construction that either do not simplify the sketch or are not required to interpret the sketch quickly and accurately.

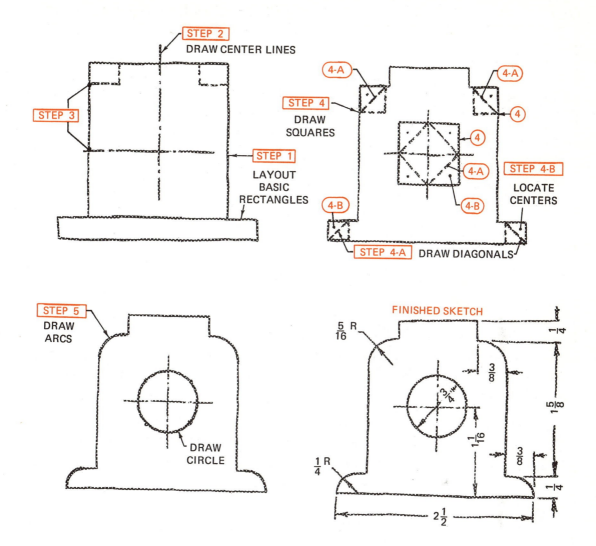

FIGURE 30-2 SKETCHING AN IRREGULAR SHAPE

The techniques described in this unit have been found by tested experience to be essential in training the beginner to sketch accurately.

As skill is developed in drawing straight, slant and curved lines freehand in combination with each other, some of the steps in sketching irregularly-shaped parts may be omitted and the process shortened.

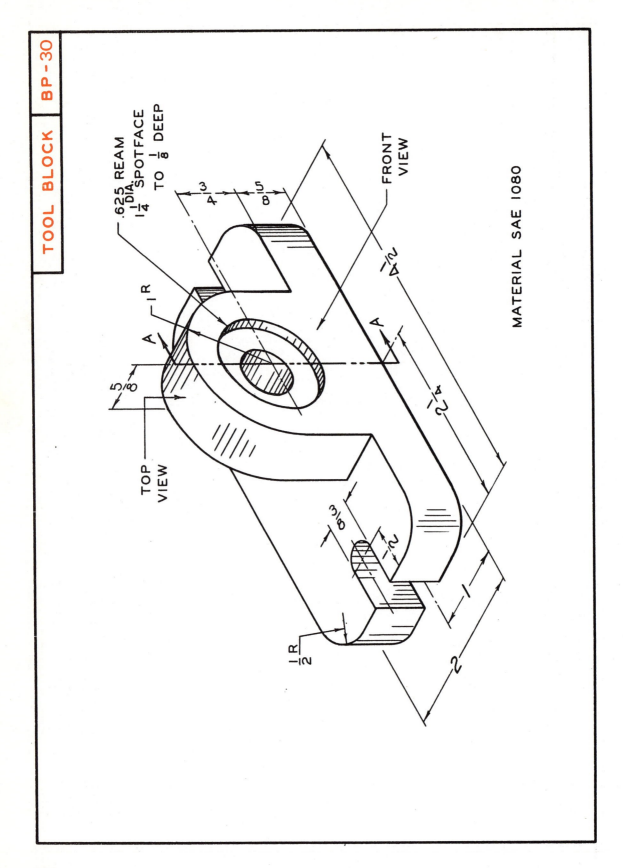

TOOL BLOCK | BP-30

.625 REAM
1¼ DIA.
SPOTFACE
TO ⅛ DEEP

FRONT VIEW

MATERIAL SAE 1080

ASSIGNMENT   UNIT 30

STUDENT'S NAME

SUGGESTIONS
① START FRONT VIEW 1" FROM LEFT BORDER
   AND 3/16 FROM BOTTOM BORDER
② ALLOW 1½" BETWEEN VIEWS

SKETCHING ASSIGNMENT FOR TOOL BLOCK (BP-30)
① MAKE A FREEHAND SKETCH OF THE
   FRONT VIEW AND TOP VIEW
② SKETCH FULL SECTION A-A
③ DIMENSION FRONT AND TOP VIEWS

UNIT 31   SKETCHING FILLETS, RADII, ROUNDED CORNERS AND EDGES

Wherever practical, sharp corners are rounded and sharp edges are eliminated. This is true of fabricated and hardened parts where a sharp corner reduces the strength of the object. It is also true of castings where sharp edges and corners may be difficult to produce, figure 31-1.

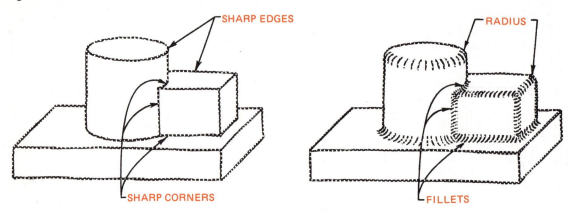

FIGURE 31-1 ELIMINATING SHARP EDGES AND CORNERS

Where an outside edge is rounded, the convex edge is called a *round edge* or *radius*. A rounded inside corner is known as a *fillet.*

SKETCHING A FILLET OR RADIUS

Regardless of whether a fillet or radius is required, the steps for sketching each one are identical. The step-by-step procedure is illustrated in figure 31-2.

	STEP 1	STEP 2	STEP 3	STEP 4
SKETCHING A FILLET				FILLET COMPLETED
SKETCHING A RADIUS				RADIUS COMPLETED

FIGURE 31-2 STEPS IN SKETCHING A FILLET OR RADIUS

STEP 1 ▶ Sketch the lines which represent the edge or corner.

STEP 2 ▶ Draw the arc to the required radius.

STEP 3 ▶ Draw two lines parallel to the edge line from the two points where the arc touches the straight lines.

STEP 4 ▶ Sketch a series of curved lines across the work with the same arc as the object line. These curved lines start at one of the parallel lines and terminate at the other end.

SKETCHING INTERSECTING RADII AND FILLETS

The method of sketching corners at which radii or fillets come together is shown in the three steps in figure 31-3.

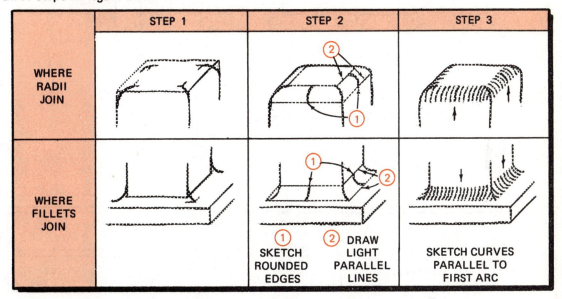

FIGURE 31-3 SKETCHING ROUNDED CORNERS AND EDGES

SKETCHING CORNERS ON CIRCULAR PARTS

The direction of radius or fillet lines changes on circular objects at a center line. The curved lines tend to straighten as they approach the center line and then slowly curve in the opposite direction beyond that point. The direction of curved lines for outside radii of round parts is shown in figure 31-4A. The curved lines for the intersecting corners are shown in figure 31-4B.

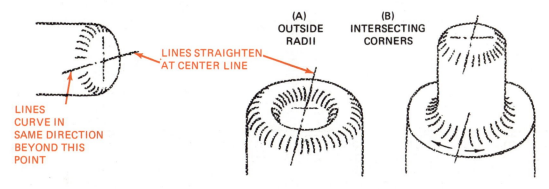

FIGURE 31-4 DIRECTION OF CURVED LINES ON ROUND PARTS

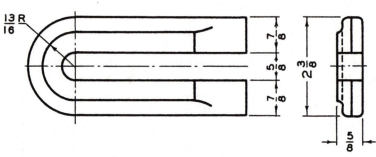

DROP FORGED STRAP | BP- 3I A

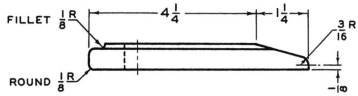

FILLET $\frac{1}{8}$R

ROUND $\frac{1}{8}$R

$\frac{13}{16}$R

$\frac{7}{8}$ $\frac{5}{8}$ $\frac{7}{8}$ $2\frac{3}{8}$

$\frac{5}{8}$

$4\frac{1}{4}$ $1\frac{1}{4}$

$\frac{3}{16}$R

$\frac{1}{8}$

ASSIGNMENT A   UNIT **31**

STUDENT'S NAME _____

SKETCHING ASSIGNMENT FOR DROP FORGED STRAP (BP- 3I A)
① COMPLETE THE SKETCH BY SHADING THE FILLETED CORNER
    AND THE ROUNDED EDGES.
② DIMENSION THE SKETCH. PLACE DIMENSIONS IN THE CIRCLES
    PROVIDED FOR THEM.

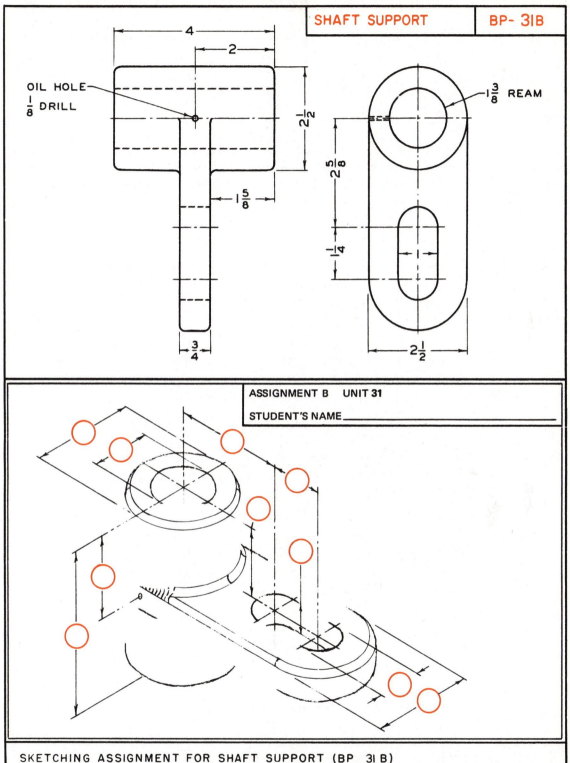

SHAFT SUPPORT | **BP- 31B**

OIL HOLE $\frac{1}{8}$ DRILL

$1\frac{3}{8}$ REAM

ASSIGNMENT B   UNIT **31**

STUDENT'S NAME_____

SKETCHING ASSIGNMENT FOR SHAFT SUPPORT (BP 31 B)
① COMPLETE THE SKETCH AND SHADE THE ROUNDED CORNERS AND FILLET.
② DIMENSION THE SKETCH. PLACE DIMENSIONS IN CIRCLES
      PROVIDED FOR THEM.

The true shape of a part or mechanism may be described accurately on a drawing by using combinations of lines and views. Added to these are the lettering, which supplies additional information, and the dimensions. For exceptionally accurate work and to standardize the shape and size of the letters, the lettering is done with a guide. In most other cases, the letters are formed freehand.

An almost square style letter known as *Gothic lettering* is very widely used because it is legible and the individual letters are simple enough to be made quickly and accurately. Gothic letters may be either vertical (straight) or inclined (slant), and upper or lower case.

FORMING UPPER CASE LETTERS

The shape of each vertical letter (both upper and lower case) and each number will be discussed in this unit. All of these letters and numbers are formed by combining vertical, horizontal, slant, and curved lines. The upper case letters should be started first as they are easiest to make.

Very light guide lines should be used to keep the letters straight and of uniform height. A soft pencil is recommended for lettering because it is possible to guide the pencil easily to form good letters.

LETTERS FORMED WITH
VERTICAL AND HORIZONTAL LINES

LETTERS FORMED WITH VERTICAL, HORIZONTAL AND SLANT LINES

LETTERS FORMED WITH STRAIGHT AND CURVED LINES

FIGURE 32-1 FORMING UPPER CASE LETTERS

The shape of each vertical letter and number is given in figures 32-1, 32-2, and 32-3. The light lines with arrows which appear with every letter give the direction and number of the strokes needed to form the letter. The small numbers indicate the sequence of the strokes. Note that most letters are narrower than they are long. Lettering is usually done with a single stroke to keep the line weight of each letter uniform.

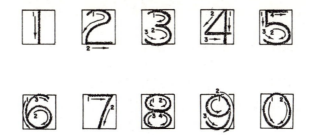

FIGURE 32-2 FORMING VERTICAL NUMERALS

SPACING LETTERS

To achieve good lettering, attention must be given to the proper spacing between letters, words and lines. Words and lines that are either condensed and run together or spread out are difficult to read, cause inaccuracies, and detract from an otherwise good drawing.

The space between letters should be about one-fourth the width of a regular letter. For example, the slant line of the letter 'A' should be one-quarter letter width away from the top line of the letter 'T'. Judgment must be used in the amount of white space left between letters so that it is as equal as possible. The letters will then look in balance and will be easy to read.

Between words, a space two-thirds the full width of a normal letter should be used. Lines of lettering are easiest to read when a space of from one-half to the full height of the letters is left between the lines.

LOWER CASE VERTICAL LETTERS

Lower case vertical letters are formed in a manner different from that used to form upper case letters. The main portion, or body, of most Gothic lower case letters is approximately the same width and height. The parts that extend above or below the body are one-half the height of the body. The shape of each vertical lower case letter and the forming of the letters are indicated in figure 32-3.

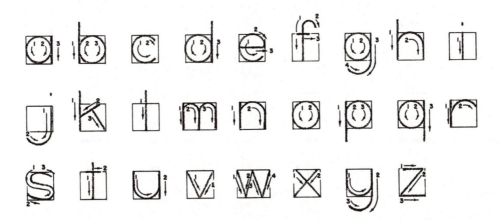

FIGURE 32-3 FORMING VERTICAL LOWER-CASE LETTERS

The spacing between lower case letters and words is the same as for capitals. The spacing between lines should be equal to the height of the body of the lower case letter to allow for the lines extending above and below the body of certain letters.

LETTERING FRACTIONS

Since fractions are important, they must not be subordinate to any of the lettering. The height of each number in the numerator and denominator must be at least two-thirds the height of a whole number. The dividing line of the fraction is in the center of the whole number. There must be a space between the numerator, the division sign, and the denominator so that neither number touches the line, figure 32-4.

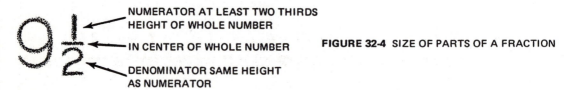

NUMERATOR AT LEAST TWO THIRDS
HEIGHT OF WHOLE NUMBER

IN CENTER OF WHOLE NUMBER   **FIGURE 32-4** SIZE OF PARTS OF A FRACTION

DENOMINATOR SAME HEIGHT
AS NUMERATOR

LETTERING RIGHT OR LEFT HANDED

The forming of letters to this point has been in terms of lettering with the right hand. Analysis of the steps followed in lettering with the left hand shows that the strokes are often reversed. Figure 32-5 may be used as a guide for forming letters with the left hand.

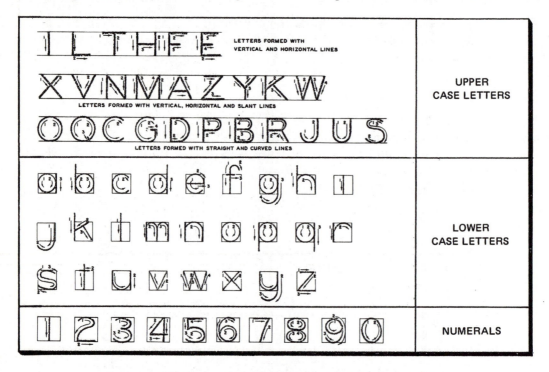

FIGURE 32-5 FORMING VERTICAL LETTERS WITH THE LEFT HAND

The beginner should pay very close attention to the proper forming of letters, uniform line weights, and correct spacing. Once these skills have been mastered speed in lettering can be gained by continual practice in lettering words and sentences freehand.

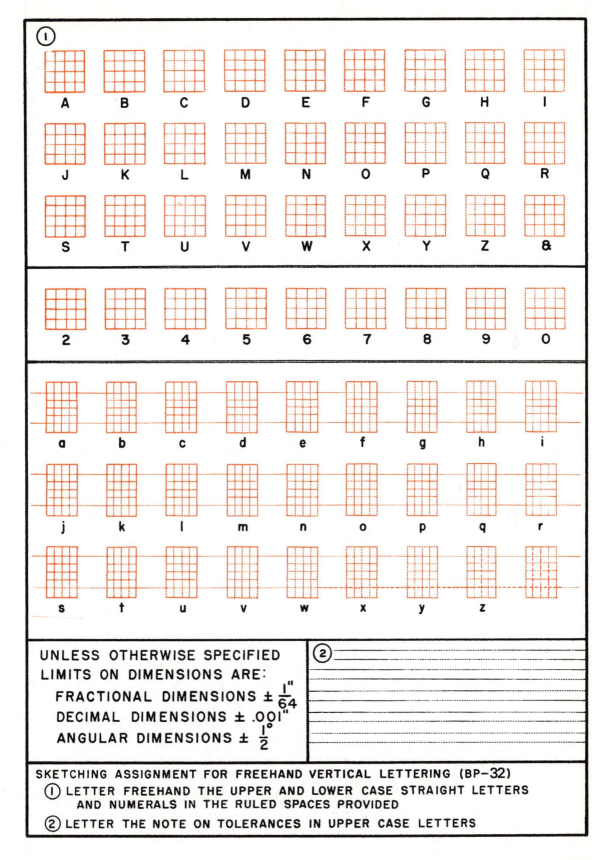

A B C D E F G H I

J K L M N O P Q R

S T U V W X Y Z &

2 3 4 5 6 7 8 9 0

a b c d e f g h i

j k l m n o p q r

s t u v w x y z

UNLESS OTHERWISE SPECIFIED
LIMITS ON DIMENSIONS ARE:
  FRACTIONAL DIMENSIONS ± $\frac{1}{64}$"
  DECIMAL DIMENSIONS ± .001"
  ANGULAR DIMENSIONS ± $\frac{1}{2}$°

SKETCHING ASSIGNMENT FOR FREEHAND VERTICAL LETTERING (BP-32)
  ① LETTER FREEHAND THE UPPER AND LOWER CASE STRAIGHT LETTERS
     AND NUMERALS IN THE RULED SPACES PROVIDED
  ② LETTER THE NOTE ON TOLERANCES IN UPPER CASE LETTERS

Inclined letters and numbers are used on many drawings as they can be formed with a very natural movement and a slant similar to that used in everyday writing. The shape of the inclined or slant letter is the same as that of the vertical or straight letter except that circles and parts of circles are elliptical and the axis of each letter is at an angle, figure 33-1. Slant letters may be formed with the left hand using the same techniques of shaping and spacing as are used by the right hand. The only difference is that for some letters and numerals the strokes are reversed.

LETTERS FORMED WITH SLANT AND HORIZONTAL LINES

LETTERS FORMED WITH SLANT LINES

LETTERS FORMED WITH CURVED AND SLANT LINES

FIGURE 33-1 FORMING UPPER CASE SLANT LETTERS

FORMING SLANT LETTERS AND NUMERALS

The angle of slant of the letters and numerals may vary, depending on individual preference. Lettering at an angle of from 60 to 75 degrees is practical, as it is easy to read and produce. Light horizontal guide lines to assure the uniform height of letters are recommended for the beginner. Angle guide lines assist the beginner in keeping all the letters shaped correctly and spaced properly. The direction of the strokes for each letter and numeral, and the spacing between letters, words, and lines are the same as for straight letters. The shape of each upper case slant letter is illustrated in figure 33-1; each numeral is shown in figure 33-2; and each lower case slant letter is shown in figure 33-3.

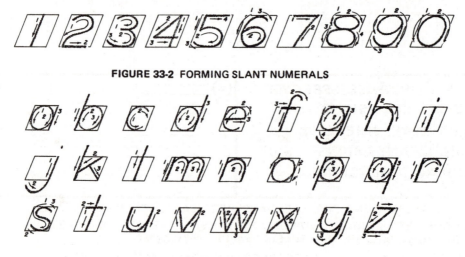

FIGURE 33-2 FORMING SLANT NUMERALS

FIGURE 33-3 FORMING LOWER CASE SLANT LETTERS

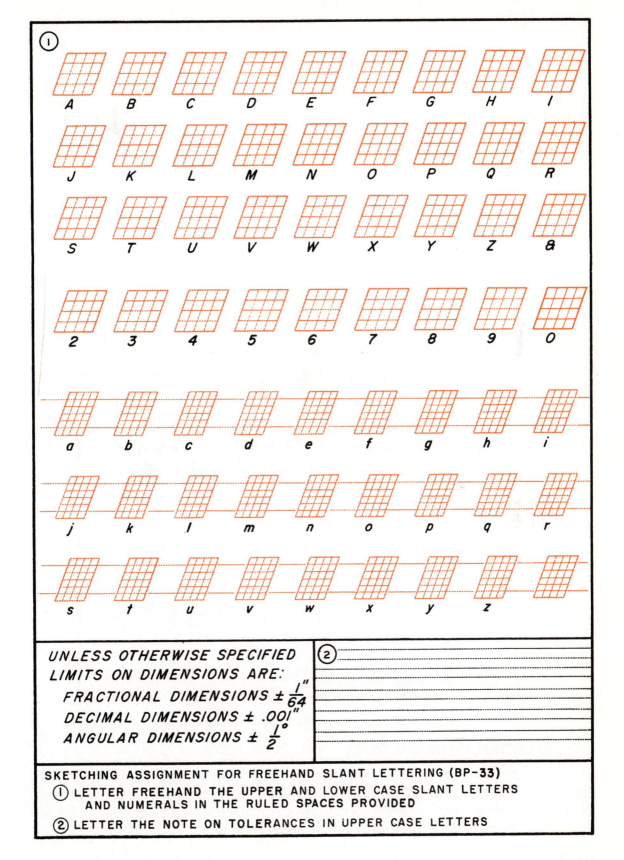

① A B C D E F G H I

J K L M N O P Q R

S T U V W X Y Z 8

2 3 4 5 6 7 8 9 0

a b c d e f g h i

j k l m n o p q r

s t u v w x y z

UNLESS OTHERWISE SPECIFIED
LIMITS ON DIMENSIONS ARE:
FRACTIONAL DIMENSIONS $\pm \frac{1}{64}"$
DECIMAL DIMENSIONS $\pm .001"$
ANGULAR DIMENSIONS $\pm \frac{1}{2}°$

②

SKETCHING ASSIGNMENT FOR FREEHAND SLANT LETTERING (BP-33)

① LETTER FREEHAND THE UPPER AND LOWER CASE SLANT LETTERS
   AND NUMERALS IN THE RULED SPACES PROVIDED

② LETTER THE NOTE ON TOLERANCES IN UPPER CASE LETTERS

PICTORIAL DRAWINGS

Pictorial drawings are very easy to understand because they show an object as it appears to the person viewing it. Pictorial drawings show the length, width, and height of an object in a single view. The use of a pictorial drawing enables an individual, inexperienced in interpreting drawings, to visualize quickly the shape of single parts or various components in a complicated mechanism.

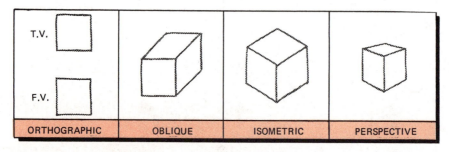

FIGURE 34-1 FOUR COMMON TYPES OF SKETCHES

There are three general types of pictorial drawings in common use: ① oblique, ② isometric and ③ perspective. A fourth type of freehand drawing is the orthographic sketch, figure 34-1. The advantages and general principles of making orthographic sketches are described in this unit.

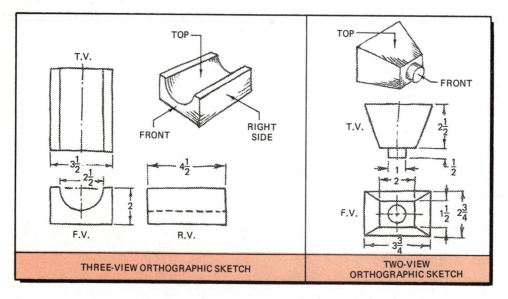

FIGURE 34-2 EXAMPLES OF ORTHOGRAPHIC SKETCHES

MAKING ORTHOGRAPHIC SKETCHES

The orthographic sketch is the simplest type to make of the four types of sketches. The views are developed as in any regular mechanical drawing and the same types of lines are used. The only difference is that orthographic sketches are drawn freehand. In actual practice, on-the-spot sketches of small parts are made as near the actual size as possible.

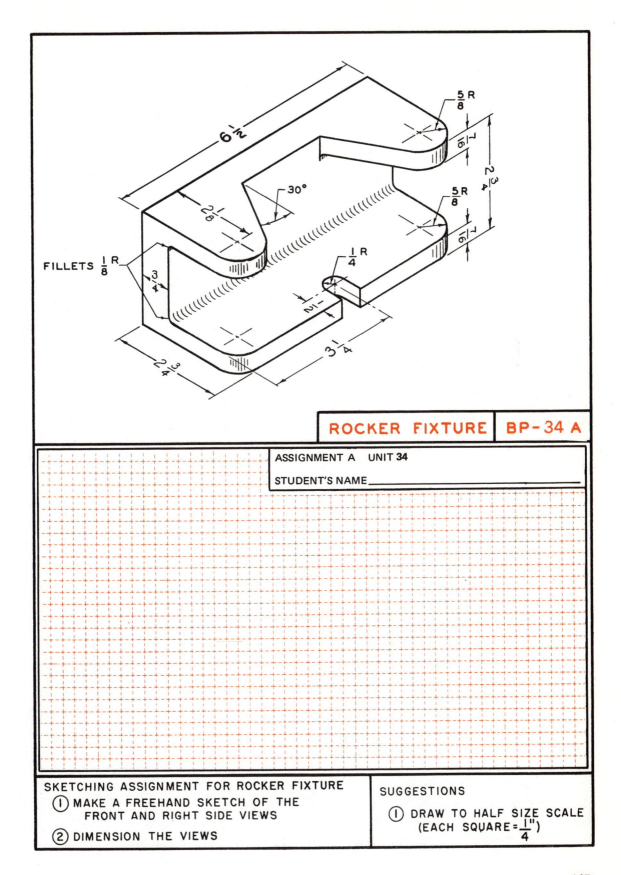

$6\frac{1}{2}$

$\frac{5}{8}$ R

$\frac{7}{16}$

$2\frac{3}{4}$

$30°$

$2\frac{1}{8}$

$\frac{5}{8}$ R

$\frac{7}{16}$

FILLETS $\frac{1}{8}$ R

$\frac{3}{4}$

$\frac{1}{4}$ R

$\frac{1}{2}$

$\frac{1}{2}$

$3\frac{1}{4}$

$2\frac{3}{4}$

ROCKER FIXTURE | **BP- 34 A**

ASSIGNMENT A   UNIT **34**

STUDENT'S NAME_____

SKETCHING ASSIGNMENT FOR ROCKER FIXTURE

① MAKE A FREEHAND SKETCH OF THE
   FRONT AND RIGHT SIDE VIEWS

② DIMENSION THE VIEWS

SUGGESTIONS

① DRAW TO HALF SIZE SCALE
   (EACH SQUARE=$\frac{1}{4}$")

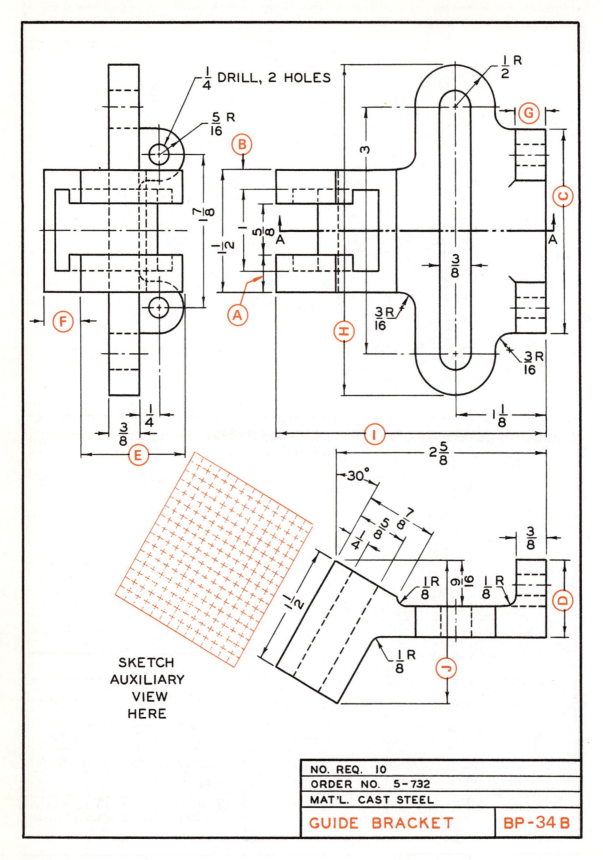

$\frac{1}{4}$ DRILL, 2 HOLES

$\frac{5}{16}$ R

$\frac{1}{2}$ R

B

G

$1\frac{7}{8}$

$1\frac{1}{2}$

$\frac{5}{8}$

3

C

A

A

$\frac{3}{8}$

F

$\frac{3 R}{16}$

$\frac{3 R}{16}$

H

$\frac{3}{8}$

$\frac{1}{4}$

$1\frac{1}{8}$

E

I

$2\frac{5}{8}$

30°

$\frac{7}{8}$

$\frac{5}{8}$

$\frac{1}{4}$

$\frac{3}{8}$

$1\frac{1}{2}$

$\frac{1}{8}$ R

$\frac{9}{16}$

$\frac{1}{8}$ R

D

$\frac{1}{8}$ R

J

SKETCH
AUXILIARY
VIEW
HERE

NO. REQ. 10	
ORDER NO. 5-732	
MAT'L. CAST STEEL	
GUIDE BRACKET	**BP-34 B**

ASSIGNMENT B   UNIT **34**

STUDENT'S NAME _____

SKETCHING ASSIGNMENT FOR GUIDE BRACKET (BP–34B)

(1) SKETCH FREEHAND THE REQUIRED AUXILIARY VIEW IN THE SPACE PROVIDED

(2) SKETCH FREEHAND AND DIMENSION FULL SECTION VIEW A–A

GUIDE BRACKET (BP-34B)

1. Name each of the three views.

2. Give the number and diameter of the drilled holes.

3. Determine dimensions Ⓐ and Ⓑ .

4. Compute dimension Ⓒ .

5. What is the dimension of the leg Ⓓ ?

6. Compute dimension Ⓔ .

7. Give dimension Ⓕ and Ⓖ .

8. What is the overall length of Ⓗ ?

9. Determine overall height of Ⓘ .

10. Give overall width of Ⓙ .

ASSIGNMENT   UNIT 34

Student's Name _____

1. _____ , _____ , _____

2. No. _____ Diam. _____

3. Ⓐ = _____   Ⓑ = _____

4. Ⓒ = _____

5. Ⓓ = _____

6. Ⓔ = _____

7. Ⓕ = _____   Ⓖ = _____

8. Ⓗ = _____

9. Ⓘ = _____

10. Ⓙ = _____

An oblique sketch is a type of pictorial drawing on which two or more surfaces are shown at one time on one drawing. The front face of the object is sketched in the same manner as the front view of either an orthographic sketch or a mechanical drawing. All of the straight, inclined, and curved lines on the front plane of the object will appear in their true size and shape on this front face. Since the other sides of the object are sketched at an angle, the surfaces and lines are not shown in their true size and shape.

MAKING OBLIQUE SKETCHES WITH STRAIGHT LINES

The steps in making an oblique sketch are simple. For example, if an oblique sketch of a rectangular die block is needed, seven basic steps are followed as shown in figure 35-1.

STEP 1 ▶ Select one view of the object that gives most of the desired information.

STEP 2 ▶ Draw light horizontal and vertical base lines.

STEP 3 ▶ Lay out the edges of the die block in the front view from the base lines. All vertical lines on the front face of the object will be parallel to the vertical base line; all horizontal lines will be parallel to the horizontal base line. All lines will be in their true size and shape in this view.

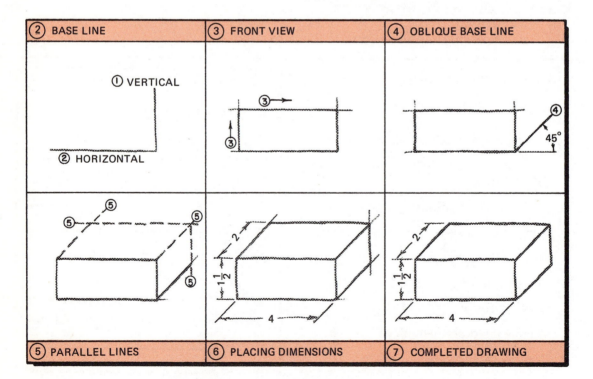

FIGURE 35-1 STEPS IN MAKING AN OBLIQUE SKETCH

STEP 4 ▶ Start at the intersection of the vertical and horizontal base lines and draw a line at an angle of 45° to the base line. This line is called the *oblique base line.*

STEP 5 ▶ Draw the remaining lines for the right side and top view parallel to either the oblique base line, or to the horizontal or vertical base lines, as the case may be. Since these lines are not in their true size or shape, they should be drawn so they appear in proportion to the front view.

STEP 6 ▶ Place dimensions so they are parallel to the axis lines.

STEP 7 ▶ Erase unnecessary lines. Darken object lines to make the sketch clearer and easier to interpret.

SKETCHING CIRCLES IN OBLIQUE

A circle or arc located on the front face of an oblique sketch is drawn in its true size and shape. However, since the top and side views are distorted, a circle or arc will be elliptical in these views. Three circles drawn in oblique on the top, right side, and front of a cube are shown in figure 35-2.

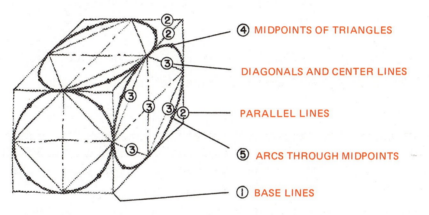

④ MIDPOINTS OF TRIANGLES

DIAGONALS AND CENTER LINES

PARALLEL LINES

⑤ ARCS THROUGH MIDPOINTS

① BASE LINES

FIGURE 35-2 SKETCHING CIRCLES IN OBLIQUE

STEP 1 ▶ Draw horizontal, vertical, and oblique base lines.

STEP 2 ▶ Sketch lines parallel to these base lines or *axes* to form a cube.

STEP 3 ▶ Draw center lines and diagonals in the front, right side, and top faces.

STEP 4 ▶ Locate the midpoints of triangles formed in the three faces.

STEP 5 ▶ Draw curved lines through these points. NOTE: The circle appears in its true size and shape in the front face, and as an ellipse in the right side and top faces.

STEP 6 ▶ Touch up and darken the curved lines. Erase guidelines where they are of no value in reading the sketch.

RIGHT AND LEFT OBLIQUE SKETCHES

Up to this point, the object has been viewed from the right side. In many cases, the left side of the object must be sketched because it contains better details. In these instances, the oblique base line or axis is 45° from the horizontal base line, starting from the left edge of the object. A rectangular die block sketched from the right side is shown in figure 35-3A. The same rectangular die block is shown in figure 35-3B as it would appear when sketched from the left side.

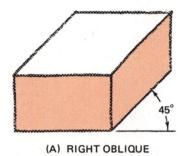
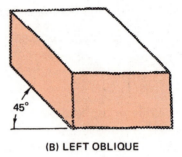

(A) RIGHT OBLIQUE   (B) LEFT OBLIQUE

FIGURE 35-3 RIGHT AND LEFT OBLIQUE SKETCHES

The same principles and techniques of making oblique sketches apply, regardless of whether the object is drawn in the right or left position.

FORESHORTENING

When a line in the side and top views is drawn in the same proportion as lines are in the front view, the object may appear to be distorted and longer than it actually is. To correct the distortion, the lines are drawn shorter than actual size so the sketch of the part looks balanced. This drafting technique is called *foreshortening.*

In figure 35-4, the oblique sketch shows a part as it would look before and after foreshortening. The foreshortened version is preferred. The amount the sketch is foreshortened depends on the ability of the individual to make the sketch resemble the part as closely as possible.

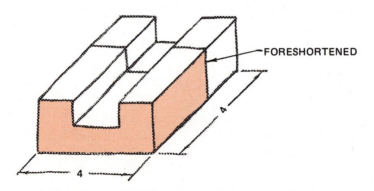

FIGURE 35-4 FORESHORTENING CORRECTS DISTORTION

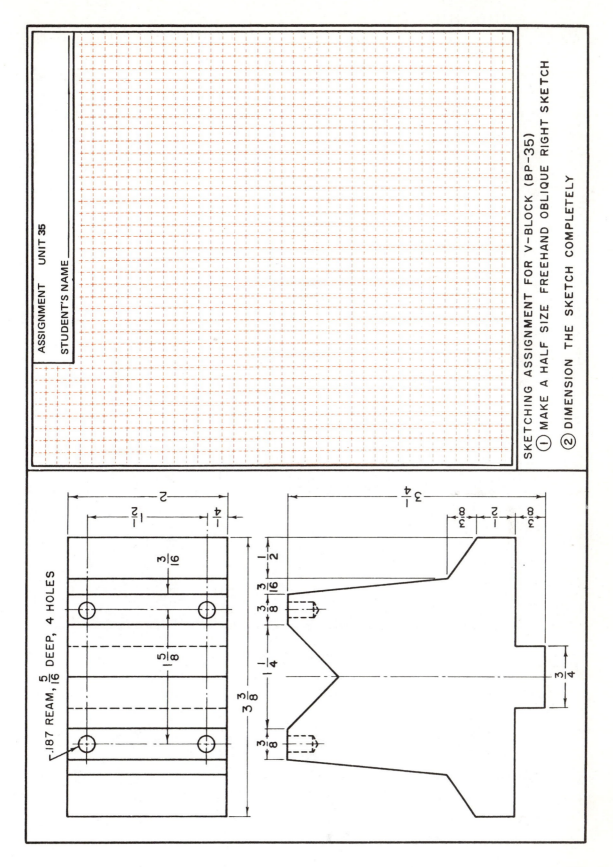

ASSIGNMENT   UNIT 35

STUDENT'S NAME

SKETCHING ASSIGNMENT FOR V-BLOCK (BP-35)

① MAKE A HALF SIZE FREEHAND OBLIQUE RIGHT SKETCH

② DIMENSION THE SKETCH COMPLETELY

Isometric and oblique sketches are similar in that they are another form of pictorial drawing in which two or more surfaces may be illustrated in one view. The isometric sketch is built around three major lines called isometric base lines or axes, figure 36-1. The right side and left side isometric base lines each form an angle of 30° with the horizontal, and the vertical axis line forms an angle of 90° with the horizontal base line.

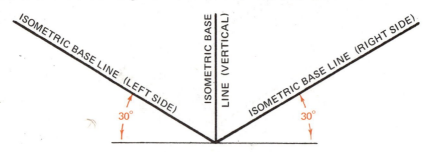

FIGURE 36-1 AXES FOR ISOMETRIC DRAWINGS

MAKING A SIMPLE ISOMETRIC SKETCH

An object is sketched in isometric by positioning it so that the part seems to rest on one corner. When making an isometric sketch of a part where all the surfaces or corners are parallel or at right angles to each other, the basic steps used are shown in figure 36-2. A rectangular steel block 1″ thick, 2″ wide, and 3″ long is used as an example.

① LAYOUT AXES	② MEASURING ALONG AXES	③ DRAWING PARALLEL LINES	④ DIMENSIONING
30° 30°			1 2 3

FIGURE 36-2 STEPS IN MAKING AN ISOMETRIC SKETCH

STEP 1 ▶ Sketch the three isometric axes. If a ruled isometric sheet is available, select three lines for the major axes.

STEP 2 ▶ Lay off the 3″ length along the right axis, the 2″ width on the left axis line, and the 1″ height on the vertical axis line.

STEP 3 ▶ Draw lines from these layout points parallel to the three axes. Note that all parallel lines on the object are parallel on the sketch.

STEP 4 ▶ Dimension the sketch. On isometric sketches, the dimensions are placed parallel to the edges.

SKETCHING SLANT LINES IN ISOMETRIC

Only those lines that are parallel to the axes may be measured in their true lengths. Slant lines representing inclined surfaces are not shown in their true lengths in isometric sketches. In most cases, the slant lines for an object (such as the casting shown in figure 36-3) may be drawn by following the steps shown in figure 36-4.

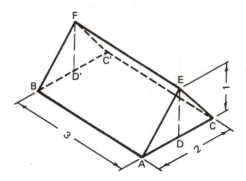

FIGURE 36-3 PART TO BE SKETCHED IN ISOMETRIC

STEP 1 ▶ Draw the three major isometric axes.

STEP 2 ▶ Measure distance AB on the left axis and AC on the right axis.

STEP 3 ▶ Measure distance AD on the right axis and draw a vertical line from this point. Lay out distance DE on this line.

STEP 4 ▶ Draw parallel lines EF, BC', FD'.

STEP 5 ▶ Connect and darken lines AB, AC, AE, EC, BF, and EF.

STEP 6 ▶ Dimension the isometric sketch.

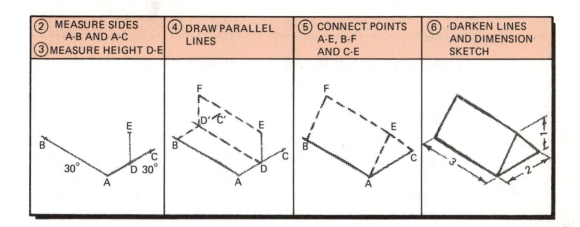

FIGURE 36-4 ISOMETRIC SKETCH REQUIRING USE OF SLANT LINES

SKETCHING CIRCLES AND ARCS IN ISOMETRIC

The techniques used to sketch arcs and circles in oblique also may be used for sketching arcs and circles in isometric. Each step is illustrated in figure 36-5. Note that in each face the circle appears as an ellipse. This is also shown in figure 36-6.

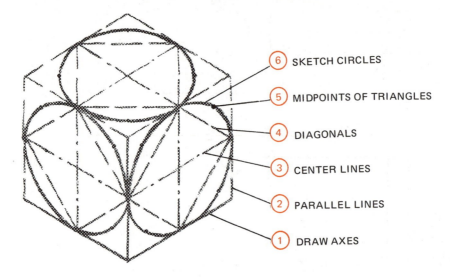

6 SKETCH CIRCLES

5 MIDPOINTS OF TRIANGLES

4 DIAGONALS

3 CENTER LINES

2 PARALLEL LINES

1 DRAW AXES

FIGURE 36-5 SKETCHING CIRCLES IN ISOMETRIC

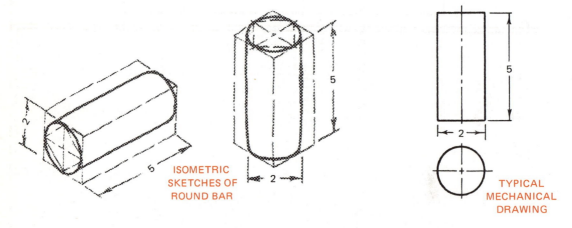

ISOMETRIC
SKETCHES OF
ROUND BAR

TYPICAL
MECHANICAL
DRAWING

FIGURE 36-6 APPLICATION OF CIRCLES AND ARCS IN ISOMETRIC

LAYOUT SHEETS FOR ISOMETRIC SKETCHES

The making of isometric drawings can be simplified if specially ruled isometric layout sheets are used. Considerable time may be saved as these graph sheets provide guide lines which run in three directions. The guide lines are parallel to the three isometric axes and to each other. The diagonal lines of the graph paper usually are at a given distance apart to simplify the making of the sketch and to ensure that all lines are in proportion to the actual size. The ruled lines are printed on a heavy paper which can be used over and over again as an underlay sheet for tracing paper.

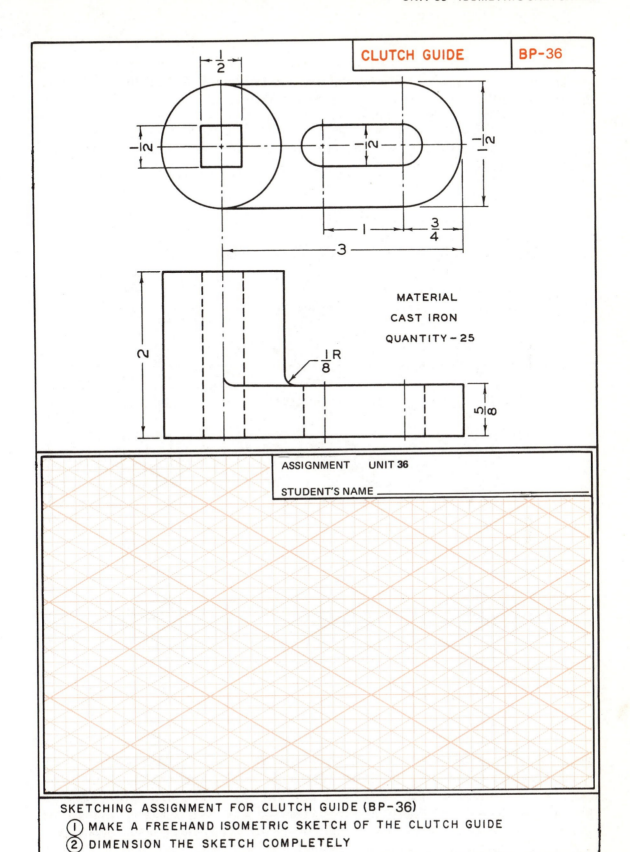

CLUTCH GUIDE   BP-36

MATERIAL
CAST IRON
QUANTITY - 25

$\frac{1}{8}$R

ASSIGNMENT   UNIT 36

STUDENT'S NAME _____

SKETCHING ASSIGNMENT FOR CLUTCH GUIDE (BP-36)
1 MAKE A FREEHAND ISOMETRIC SKETCH OF THE CLUTCH GUIDE
2 DIMENSION THE SKETCH COMPLETELY

PERSPECTIVE SKETCHING

Perspective sketches show two or three sides of an object in one view. As a result, they resemble a photographic picture. In both the perspective sketch and the photograph, the portion of the object which is closest to the observer is the largest. The parts that are farthest away are smaller. Lines and surfaces on perspective sketches become smaller and come closer together as the distance from the eye increases. Eventually they seem to disappear at an imaginary horizon.

SINGLE POINT PARALLEL PERSPECTIVE

There are two types of perspective sketches commonly used in the shop. The first type is known as *single point* or *parallel perspective.* In this case, one face of the object in parallel perspective is sketched in its true size and shape, the same as in an orthographic sketch. For example, the edges of the front face of a cube as shown in parallel perspective in figure 37-1 at (A) , (B) , (C) and (D) , are parallel and square.

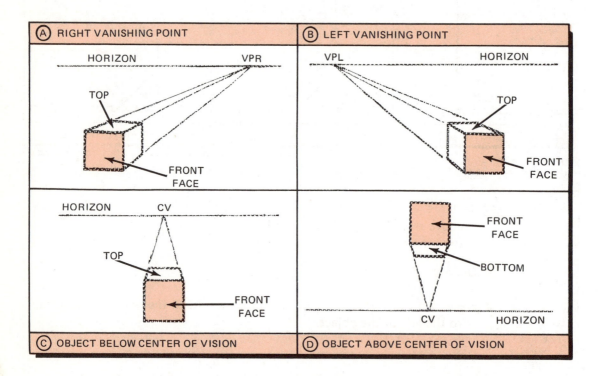

FIGURE 37-1 SINGLE POINT, PARALLEL PERSPECTIVE SKETCHES OF A CUBE

To draw the remainder of the cube, the two sides decrease in size as they approach the horizon. On this imaginary horizon, which is supposed to be at eye level, the point where the lines come together is called the *vanishing point.* This vanishing point may be above or below the object, or to the right or left of it, figure 37-1. Vertical lines on the object are vertical on parallel perspective sketches and do not converge. Single point parallel perspective is the simplest type of perspective to understand and the easiest to sketch.

ANGULAR OR TWO-POINT PERSPECTIVE

The second type of perspective sketch is the two-point perspective, also known as *angular perspective.* As the name implies, two vanishing points on the horizon are used and all lines converge toward these points. Usually, in a freehand perspective sketch, the horizon is in a horizontal position. Seven basic steps are required to make a two-point perspective of a cube, using right and left vanishing points. The application of each of these steps is shown in figure 37-2.

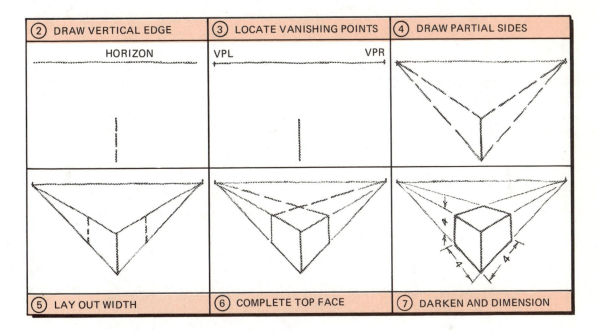

FIGURE 37-2 MAKING AN ANGULAR PERSPECTIVE SKETCH OF A CUBE

STEP 1 ▶ Sketch a light horizontal line for the horizon. Then position the object above or below this line so the right vertical edge of the cube becomes the center of the sketch.

STEP 2 ▶ Draw a vertical line for this edge of the cube.

STEP 3 ▶ Place two vanishing points on the horizon: one to the right and the other to the left of the object.

STEP 4 ▶ Draw light lines from the corners of the vertical line to the vanishing points.

STEP 5 ▶ Lay out the width of the cube and draw parallel vertical lines.

STEP 6 ▶ Sketch the two remaining lines for the top, starting at the points where the two vertical lines intersect the top edge of the cube.

STEP 7 ▶ Darken all object lines and dimension. Once again, each dimension is placed parallel to the edge which it measures.

SKETCHING CIRCLES AND ARCS IN PERSPECTIVE

Circles and arcs are distorted in all views of perspective drawings except in one face of a parallel perspective drawing. Circles are drawn in perspective, using the same techniques of blocking-in which apply to orthographic, oblique, and isometric sketches. The steps in drawing circles in perspective are summarized in figure 37-3. The same practices may be applied to sketching arcs.

STEP 1 ▶ Lay out the four sides of the square which correspond to the diameter of the required circle. Note that two of the sides converge toward the vanishing point.

STEP 2 ▶ Draw the center lines.

STEP 3 ▶ Draw the diagonals.

STEP 4 ▶ Locate the midpoints of the triangles which are formed.

STEP 5 ▶ Sketch the circle through the points where the center lines touch the sides of the square and the midpoints.

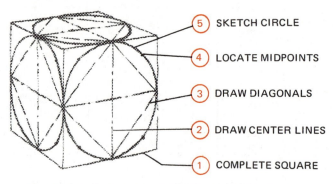

(5) SKETCH CIRCLE

(4) LOCATE MIDPOINTS

(3) DRAW DIAGONALS

(2) DRAW CENTER LINES

(1) COMPLETE SQUARE

FIGURE 37-3 SKETCHING CIRCLES IN PERSPECTIVE

SHADING PERSPECTIVE SKETCHES

Many perspective sketches are made of parts which include fillets, rounds, chamfers, and similar construction. By bringing out some of these details, the drawing becomes easier to read and is more attractive. The same techniques that are used for shading regular mechanical drawings or other pictorial sketches may be applied to perspective drawings. This shading brings out some of the construction details which otherwise might not be included, figure 37-4.

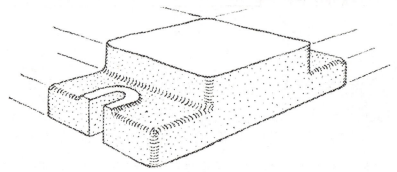

FIGURE 37-4 SHADING APPLIED TO PERSPECTIVE SKETCH OF DIE BLOCK

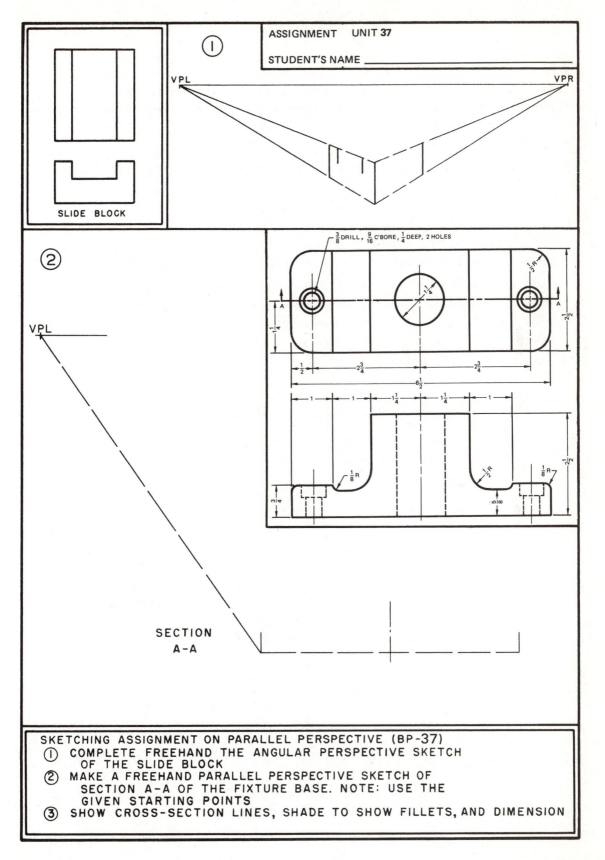

SLIDE BLOCK

ASSIGNMENT   UNIT **37**

STUDENT'S NAME _____

VPL   VPR

①

②

$\frac{3}{8}$ DRILL, $\frac{9}{16}$ C'BORE, $\frac{1}{4}$ DEEP, 2 HOLES

$\frac{1}{2}$R

$1\frac{1}{4}$

$2\frac{1}{2}$

$1\frac{1}{4}$

$\frac{1}{2}$ $2\frac{3}{4}$ $2\frac{3}{4}$

$6\frac{1}{2}$

1   1 $1\frac{1}{4}$ $1\frac{1}{4}$ 1

$\frac{1}{8}$R $\frac{1}{2}$R $\frac{1}{8}$R

$\frac{3}{4}$ $\frac{5}{8}$ $2\frac{1}{2}$

VPL

SECTION
A-A

SKETCHING ASSIGNMENT ON PARALLEL PERSPECTIVE (BP-37)
① COMPLETE FREEHAND THE ANGULAR PERSPECTIVE SKETCH
   OF THE SLIDE BLOCK
② MAKE A FREEHAND PARALLEL PERSPECTIVE SKETCH OF
   SECTION A-A OF THE FIXTURE BASE. NOTE: USE THE
   GIVEN STARTING POINTS
③ SHOW CROSS-SECTION LINES, SHADE TO SHOW FILLETS, AND DIMENSION

UNIT 38   *PICTORIAL DRAWINGS AND DIMENSIONS*

PICTORIAL WORKING DRAWINGS

Many industries, engineering, design, sales, and other organizations use pictorial working drawings that are made freehand. In a great many cases, this method is preferred to instrument drawings. Technicians are also continuously making sketches in the shop and laboratory. The sketches simplify the reading of a drawing. The fact that no drawing instruments are required and sketches may be made quickly and on-the-spot makes freehand drawings practical.

A pictorial drawing is considered a working drawing when dimensions and other specifications that are needed to produce the part or assemble a mechanism are placed on the sketch. There are two general systems of dimensioning pictorial sketches: (1) *pictorial plane* (aligned) and (2) *unidirectional.*

PICTORIAL PLANE (ALIGNED) AND UNIDIRECTIONAL DIMENSIONS

In the aligned or pictorial plane dimensioning system, the dimension lines, extension lines, and certain arrowheads are positioned parallel to the pictorial planes. These features, as they are positioned on a sketch, are illustrated in figure 38-1.

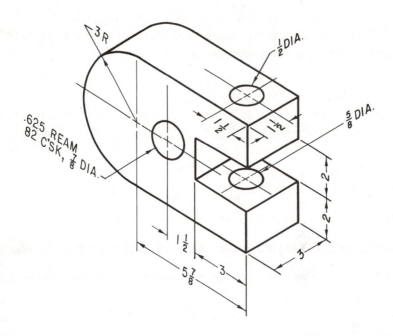

FIGURE 38-1 PICTORIAL PLANE (ALIGNED) DIMENSIONING

By contrast, dimensions, notes, and technical details are lettered vertically in unidirectional dimensioning, figure 38-2. In this vertical position the dimensions are easier to read.

160

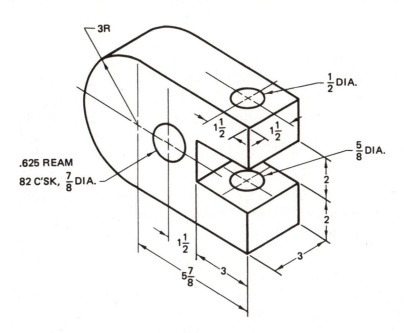

FIGURE 38-2 UNIDIRECTIONAL DIMENSIONING

Pictorial drawings are prepared according to both the United States and Metric systems of representation. Thus, the dimensions, notes, and important data as included on the sketch, conform to the standards of the system being used.

PICTORIAL DIMENSIONING RULES

Essentially, the same basic rules for dimensioning a pictorial sketch are followed as for a multiview drawing. The basic pictorial dimensioning rules apply to both the aligned and unidirectional dimensioning systems.

RULE 1 ▶ Dimensions and extension lines are drawn parallel to the pictorial planes.

RULE 2 ▶ Dimensions are placed on visible features whenever possible.

RULE 3 ▶ Arrowheads lie in the same plane as extension and dimension lines.

RULE 4 ▶ Notes and dimensions are lettered parallel with the horizontal plane.

Since a pictorial drawing is a one-view drawing, it is not always possible to avoid dimensioning on the object, across dimension lines, or on hidden surfaces. These practices should be avoided in order to prevent errors in reading dimensions or interpreting particular features of the part.

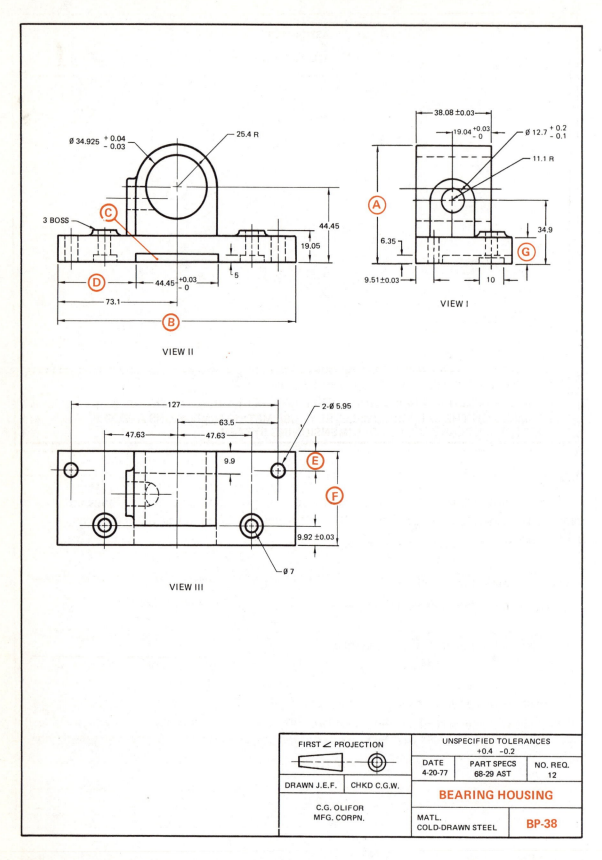

Ø 34.925 +0.04 −0.03   25.4 R

3 BOSS

C

44.45

19.05

D   44.45 +0.03 −0

5

73.1

B

VIEW II

38.08 ±0.03

19.04 +0.03 −0   Ø 12.7 +0.2 −0.1

11.1 R

A

34.9

6.35

G

9.51±0.03   10

VIEW I

127

63.5

47.63   47.63   2-Ø 5.95

9.9

E

F

9.92 ±0.03

Ø 7

VIEW III

FIRST ∠ PROJECTION		UNSPECIFIED TOLERANCES +0.4 −0.2		
		DATE 4-20-77	PART SPECS 68-29 AST	NO. REQ. 12
DRAWN J.E.F.	CHKD C.G.W.	BEARING HOUSING		
C.G. OLIFOR MFG. CORPN.		MATL. COLD-DRAWN STEEL		BP-38

ASSIGNMENT   UNIT **38**

STUDENT'S NAME _____

SKETCHING ASSIGNMENT FOR BEARING HOUSING (BP-38)
① MAKE A FREEHAND ISOMETRIC SKETCH OF THE BEARING HOUSING.
② DIMENSION THE SKETCH COMPLETELY. USE METRIC DIMENSIONS AND THE
   PICTORIAL PLANE (ALIGNED) DIMENSIONING SYSTEM.

---

1. State what angle of projection is used.

2. Name Views I, Ii, and III.

3. Compute maximum overall height
    Ⓐ

4. Determine the lower limit of Ⓑ .

5. Determine the maximum height and
    depth of slot Ⓒ .

6. Determine the maximum distance
    Ⓓ .

7. Compute the minimum and maximum
    center line distance Ⓔ .

8. Compute the maximum overall width
    Ⓕ .

9. What does the oval hole in View III
    represent?

10. Give the specifications for the counter-
    bored holes.

ASSIGNMENT   UNIT 38

Student's Name _____

1. _____

2. I = _____   II = _____

    III = _____

3. Ⓐ = _____ 4. Ⓑ = _____

5. Ⓒ = _____

    _____

6. Ⓓ = _____

7. Ⓔ = _____ _____

8. Ⓕ = _____

9. _____

10. _____

INDEX